PURE Fuel

First published in 1996
by Booth-Clibborn Editions
12 Percy Street
London W1P 9FB
Design Editor : Liz Farrelly

Printed and bound in Hong Kong
by Toppan Printing Co

Published and distributed
in the United Kingdom.
Direct mail rights in Europe:
Internos Books
12 Percy Street
London W1P 9FB

Pure Fuel Concept, art direction, design : **Fuel**
Peter Miles   Damon Murray   Stephen Sorrell

Text : Richard Preston

Preface

Anyone can copy, few can create.

The world today is over-subscribed with visual images. What in life truly inspires us, or at least moves us to re-think our position? People are becoming blind to the messages which bombard them daily.

Vision is about where we want to get to, not what we expect to find. It is time to focus on that which inspires and challenges you.

Images should have clarity and focus and should move you to think and re-think. The future will return to the pure things in life because we cannot continue to deal with this bombardment of images. Cut out all the visual wallpaper to get to the core of pure inspiration.

Roy Edmondson
Levi Strauss UK Limited

8

Introduction

In a society which favours the written word for the dissemination of ideas and opinions, the visual is easily misconstrued as mere decoration.

Produced by the graphic design group Fuel - Peter Miles, Damon Murray and Stephen Sorrell - Pure Fuel is a publication which encourages the audience to form its own opinion on the content. By juxtaposing unexplained, or simply inexplicable, visual and verbal fragments they orchestrate an ambiguous manifesto in an attempt to reanimate the act of reading. Meaning, whether communicated through words or pictures, is never simply fixed.

Their art direction mixes elements of the everyday and the shocking, which leave the viewer alternately confused and enlightened. Fuel turn an unflinching mirror on to their environment, via creative work commissioned from a close circle of contemporaries; they look at society from new or alternative perspectives, encouraging debate through controversy and humour.

Pure is concerned with extremes. The eccentricity of aspirations and the banality of leisure time. Peculiar objects that exist and products that are pure fiction but close to reality. Hidden truths are revealed.

The following sixteen pages introduce the thought processes behind Fuel and contains an outline of their development.

Issue 1 GIRL

287mm x 370mm
Spring 1991

While studying on the MA Graphic Design course at the Royal College of Art (1990-1992) Peter Miles, Damon Murray and Stephen Sorrell decided to ignore the set projects and instead set up a magazine. Choosing the name Fuel reflected their energy and drive to produce work.

Each edition of Fuel magazine tackles a four-letter word, and the first issue, Girl, excited exactly the kind of rabid reaction they were after. Fuel collated visual and verbal clichés surrounding the term 'girl', and amid accusations from fellow students that the content was 'sexist', launched their uncompromising brand of graphic design – no frills, edgy, appropriated and naive – the product of necessity as much as of aesthetic preference. Dedicated from this point to working as a group, Fuel regarded the magazine as a platform for personal work, a test-bed for ideas and approaches, funded by the profits from commercial projects. The magazine was crudely litho printed in the RCA printing department.

RCA Now

Royal College of Art magazine
210mm x 297mm
April 1991

The impact of Girl helped win Fuel the commission to design a glossy college magazine. The cover was based on the security access cards carried by all students and staff members.

Diesel catalogues

315mm x 315mm
1991-1992

The bi-annual catalogues, produced by Italian jeans and sportswear company Diesel, combine highly-stylised photographic scenarios with fake vernacular typography. Commissioned from Italy, Fuel were asked to come up with and execute ideas for a number of pages. Rejecting the traditional approach of photographing clothes on models, they exploited the products' capacity as objects. Jeans were burnt as a demonstration of Fuel's sartorial preferences.

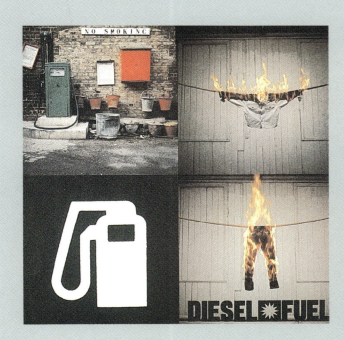

Issue 2 HYPE

210mm x 297mm
Autumn 1991

The name Fuel was starting to excite interest in wider graphic design circles. The second issue of their magazine, Hype, built upon the interest generated by Girl. It had been noted that Fuel were considered to be as uncompromising as their graphic approach, and no strangers to self-promotion. 'Fuel = Hype' spelt out in the college's windows was the first of a number of public stunts. The perforated junk-hype cardboard insert was an irritating reminder of the power of direct mail, while quotes from a televangelist told us to 'kiss the screen and make a donation'.

The mixed-media pages using screenprinting, photocopies and letterpress were hand bound. For the first time Fuel commissioned work from writers and photographers outside the college.

'The raw visual treatment has real freshness and force after a decade of sugary style in British graphic design.' *Eye*

Issue 3 USSR

1650mm x 750mm
February 1992

The force of change in Russia attracted Fuel to Moscow in early 1992. Inspired by culture shock three sheets of newsprint carried Fuel's photographs and observations, transcribed by Richard Preston. This was accompanied by an 8mm film. Yeltsin had just declared it legal to 'buy and sell anything, anywhere', and Fuel were witness to the contradictions inherent when aspirational consumerism is born in a country with no goods to sell.

To keep the budget down Fuel adopted what they much admired, the low-tech Russian approach resulting from whatever meagre means were available. USSR was printed by a local newspaper printer.

SPEC

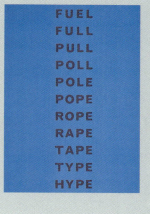

FUEL
FULL
PULL
POLL
POLE
POPE
ROPE
RAPE
TAPE
TYPE
HYPE

JUNK
HYPE

SORRY. THIS CITY IS
FUEL

Enlighten your life with **Fuel**

ТОПЛИВО 3 „МОСКВА" 15—22 ФЕВРАЛЯ 1992

„ВСЁ И ВЕЗДЕ
НА ПРОДАЖУ"

EVERYTHING EVERYWHERE IS FOR SALE

Poster installation

Virgin Records
450mm x 640mm
Winter 1991-1992

Virgin Record's Marketing department liked the magazines and commissioned an installation to be placed in the foyer of their London headquarters.

Fuel had a circular revolving light-box made which provided a billboard for a rapid turnover of ideas as A1 posters. The concept was based on a tabloid-style format focusing on topical issues. Subject matter alternated between hard political comment and flippant one-liners. Each poster set was screenprinted on to newsprint and changed every six weeks. Subjects included the dangers of over indulging on fast food, a skit on materialism and the throw-away culture of pop music.

Fuel shocked an audience which they regarded as self-consciously right-on. A healthy disregard for the brief had become a design strategy, challenging the expectations of the client.

Issue 4 CASH

258mm x 345mm
Summer 1992

Sold at the 1992 Royal College of Art Degree Show and selected gallery bookshops, the Cash issue was regarded by Fuel as the most successful realisation of their aesthetic to date. The cash-bag facsimile covers were made in the college's furniture workshops by clamping a pile of covers between two wooden blocks and drilling holes through them.

IT IS THE PERFECT
SEDUCER. IT'S PATIENT,
IT'S VERSATILE,
ENDLESSLY CHANGING
AND REGROUPING, AND
IF ACQUIRING IT WERE
NOT SO DEADLY
WE WOULD PROBABLY
CALL IT BRILLIANT.

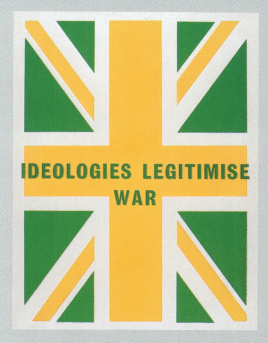

IDEOLOGIES LEGITIMISE
WAR

HAIR

CUT

Love Me

全てが欲しい

Issue 4 Summer 1992
£1
FUEL/CASH

Issue 4 Summer 1992
£5
FUEL/CASH

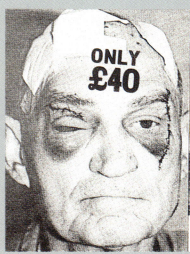

ONLY
£40

£50
A WEEK
TORY
WASTE

Pages featured a fake scratch-for-cash game, cut'n'shut cars, and a hostage barter flow chart. The mix of found and commissioned photography, illustration and writing also considered money in relation to, amongst other things, sex, the north and south regional divide and the British constitution. Printed outside the college, Cash was funded by the Virgin Records project.

'Fuel share a dislike of conventional good taste, with an editorial preference for uncomfortable, thought-provoking imagery.'
Sunday Times Magazine

West exhibition

Poster: 595mm x 840mm
Catalogue: 212mm x 280mm
July 1993

Contemporary furniture stores, E&Y in Japan and The Study in London, organised an exhibition in Tokyo showcasing young British designers. Fuel produced a catalogue which also doubled as a poster, combining David Spero's spacious landscape photography and unflinching portraiture by Peter Anderson.

Issue 5 T-shirt

265mm x 335mm
Spring / Summer 1993

'Issue 5' was a subsidiary of Fuel magazine in the form of a vacuum packed T-shirt with accompanying letterpressed insert. Text written by Mark Sinker.

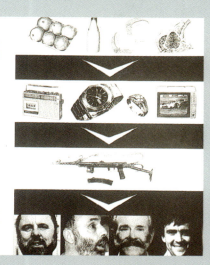

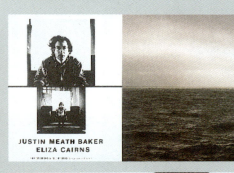

Issue 6 DEAD

200mm x 254mm
Autumn 1993

For the next issue of Fuel's magazine the most taboo of subjects was given a suitably leaden treatment within a jacket of stark black and white. The feeling behind Dead was one of refinement, subtlety and calm, a succinct sixteen pages printed on stiff white card. Light on puns and heavy on prayer-book typography, it was sombre proof of Fuel's willingness to address serious issues concerning mortality, organised religion, pollution and the dangers of fame / infamy.

Totally self-funded this issue was the first to be widely distributed by Fuel. Available mainly through art gallery bookshops in London, outlets also included shops in Paris, Amsterdam and New York.

Strangely antiseptic... scalpel sharp visual editing.' *Eye*

MTV Europe

3 x 30 seconds image spots
October 1993

Commissioned by MTV Europe, whose adventurous policy favours younger, untried directors drawn from across the cenres of visual art, this was Fuel's first effort at designing for television. Fuel chose the topics of energy conservation, fast food and hair cuts. Each spot was executed in a different media, including graphic animation, stills and live action, with a level of directness rarely seen on television.

The sequences were featured on the BBC Design Awards 1994 and also nominated for a D&AD Silver award.

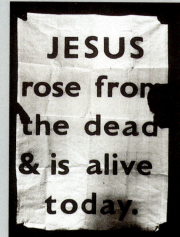

JESUS rose from the dead & is alive today.

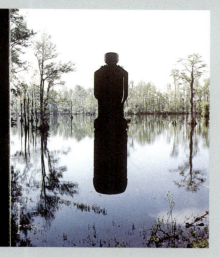

DEAD. Fuel

Save Fuel

EAT

FAST

FUEL ON HAIR M TV

Short Hair

Long Life

Fat Free

London Records magazine
480mm x 680mm
February and June 1994

The Marketing Department of London Records wanted to produce a free magazine, to be distributed in selected record shops and at the summer music festivals, with the intention of featuring and subliminally promoting the label's acts. The title, devised by Fuel, implied that this was a publication without advertising. Large-scale newsprint and a picture-led format redefined the look of the pop music publication, moving away from the cluttered columns of the weeklies and the glossy tackiness of the teen-mags. Each cover used a mixture of found photographs and graphic symbols.

Disco Inferno

Rough Trade Records
315mm x 315mm
October 1993 - August 1994

This visual identity for an indie band featured a logo of abstracted sound-waves imposed upon scenes of rural tranquillity, the implication being that the music was equally as intrusive and should be played very loud. Photography by David Spero.

Issue 7 GREY

210mm x 297mm
Autumn 1994

The word Grey, as the subject matter of the seventh Fuel magazine, provided the opportunity to discuss not simply a colour, but, on a more philosophical level, the hazy concept of the 'grey area'. At this point, ambiguity was the fundamental philosophical standpoint which Fuel themselves aspired to.

Topics predisposed to shades of greyness that were illuminated included; packaging, race, entertainment and an attack on cigarette marketing. Fuel also featured themselves in a parody of their own image, the short hair and pinstriped suits - photographed by Juergen Teller. A portrait was placed on every left-hand page to signify individuality within the mass.

The largest to date with 48 pages, each issue was stab stitched and shrink-wrapped.

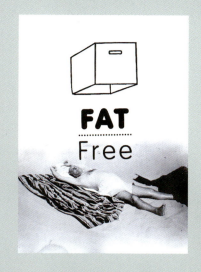

FAT
Free

ORDER   **NEW**

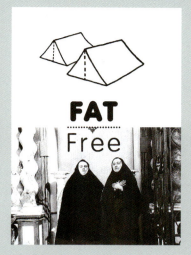

FAT
Free

Disco Inferno

GREY
Fuel

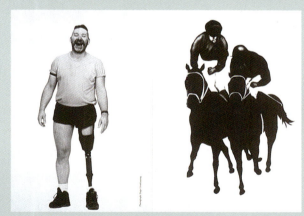

Porno
graphy
needs
you.

Grey redraws the boundaries of commercial art. This magazine has something to say beyond the process of just selling.' *Time Out*

Fuse Issue 11 Pornography

Font design: Tape Type
August 1994

The tape type alphabet was hand drawn using gaffer, hazard and insulating tape to reflect censorship.

Levi Strauss UK

Fit communication
1994-1995

Red Tab campaign
Spring 1995

After their commissions from Diesel, Fuel began a long-term working relationship with Levi's. The challenge was greater – to communicate a complex message to a diverse audience.

The Fit Communication was an attempt by the jeans company to guide buyers through the maze of products on offer. Differences in style, cut and fit were demonstrated visually using a different cloud to represent each jeans type.

The Red Tab campaign accompanied adverts by Bartle Bogle Hegarty. Fuel presented denim-clad furniture as a metaphor for each type of fit, with a hand-drawn, interlocking typeface reinforcing the theme. Photography by Matthew Donaldson.

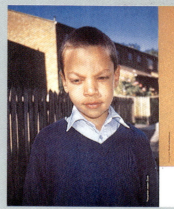

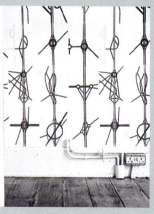

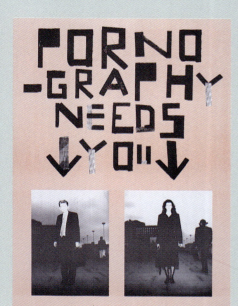

PORNO-GRAPHY NEEDS ↓YOU↓

Chit Chat

For bulls, a corridor runs between life and death. For others, the route from A to B is a lull between performances, a space for pure truth. Grey sits in such a passage, subterranean, as a table stands in a hall-way, living between scenes. An anthropologist might remark how freely gravity touches the private faces of those who pass, how their features flicker and how tics and twitches are released in transit. But Grey is immune to change, a gaze is kept low, drawn to the feet which ebb and flow around. Still as a monument. One day, Grey is no longer invisible.

Petra Ferguson

regular

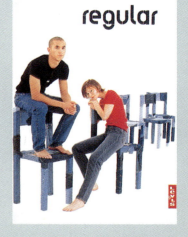

regular

Levi's
FIT Guide
Spring & Fall 1995

Discover
your
true
fit

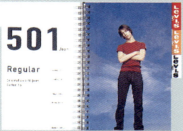

501
Regular

relaxed

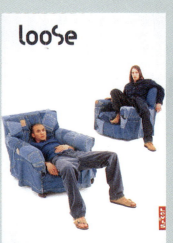

looSe

regular 505

relaxed 517

looSe 508

Time Out advertising

February and September 1995

For a series of adverts intended to promote the London listings magazine to a younger audience Fuel chose to illustrate the night-club section. These images present a picture of night-life that is both glamorous and ugly, wild and desperate. Originally intended to appear only in the limited-circulation style magazines, reaction to the campaign was so strong that poster versions were later pasted all over the city. This was followed by a second advert highlighting Time Out's restaurant coverage. Photography by Annabel Elston.

MTV Worm conference

September 1995

A prestigious conference – WORM (Word Of Relevant Mouth) – organised by MTV, and attended by advertising, marketing and design professionals from across Europe and America, addressed the issue of selling to the youth market.

Fuel were asked to produce an identity that could be applied to publicity material, stationery, signage and the conference stage. The cartoon teenager with a head full of static and the contents of a speech bubble reminiscent of an internet address spelt out just how crucial television and computer communication is to the targeted generation. Symbols designed to represent each speaker were animated on video and published in an accompanying handbook.

Tango internet advertising

October 1995

The concept of advertising on the internet may still be in its infancy, but the rapid proliferation of 'home pages' posted by commercial organisations has quickly led to designers becoming involved in the aesthetics of the interface. Offering this select on-line audience an interactive entertainment experience, imbued with the level of madness synonymous with Tango, Fuel used moving graphics to visualise numerous scripted scenarios including a hoax dating service and four hypnosis sequences.

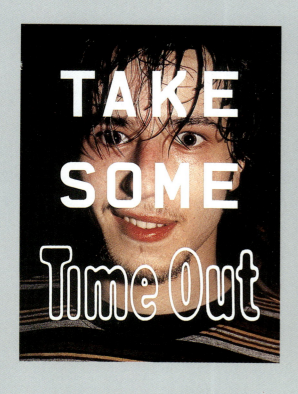

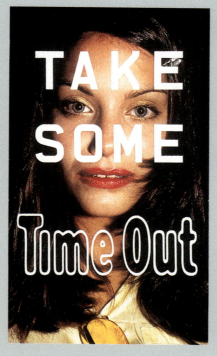

THE MUSIC IS THE MESSAGE
– THE MESSAGE IS THE MEDIUM

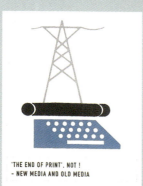

'THE END OF PRINT', NOT !
– NEW MEDIA AND OLD MEDIA

ADVERTISING IS DEAD BUT CONTINUES TO GRIN

HUMANITY IS ANALOG

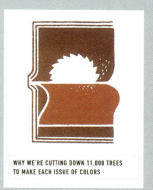

WHY WE'RE CUTTING DOWN 11,000 TREES
TO MAKE EACH ISSUE OF COLORS

W...or......m...

Brent HANSEN

Ann CLURMAN

Oliviero TOSCANI

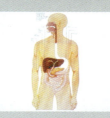

Foreword

Pure

Silver

A straight line

Smooth

Mondrian

Kim Novak's hair

A circle

The fight - 'Marvellous' Marvin Hagler versus

Tommy 'Hit-Man' Hearns, April 15th 1985

White

Brancusi

Black

Kendo Nagasaki

Johnny Haynes

Miles Davis

Fire

Water

Blue

I am almost equally a painter and a designer.

Disparate artistic disciplines seem to intercross now.
The barriers are down.

The interchange between young artists is exciting
and a book like this becomes possible because of it.
The magazines which Fuel have produced are hard to
place, there is a hint of Futurism, perhaps a touch of
Duchamp, but they are really unlike anything else.
They seem to me to be completely original, and this is
a fascinating book.

Peter Blake
London, February 8th 1996

Contents

Chapter 1

Function

Through the palm trees and down the cliff, but if we don't hurry we'll miss the train. On the sledge we have boxes of tinned pineapples stacked three deep, everything we need, and there is a bakery somewhere because we can all smell bread. Little stones keep catching the wheels. Though we are running and pulling we have no traction. Everyone else has boots but I have sandals with a small gold buckle. My soles are too smooth. If I let go I will fall in the mud, but I kick with my feet and swim and suddenly I am past all of them, swimming fast just above the surface of the field. I should be somewhere else. I should have taken the book, the pile of books, ancient and gold-leafed, to the house.

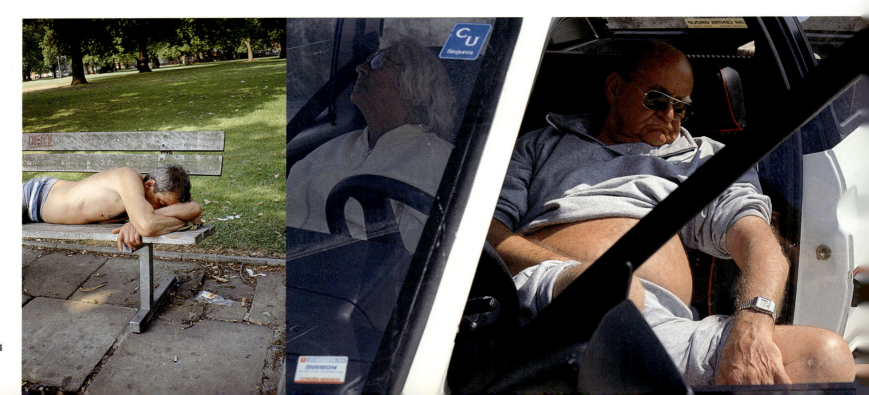

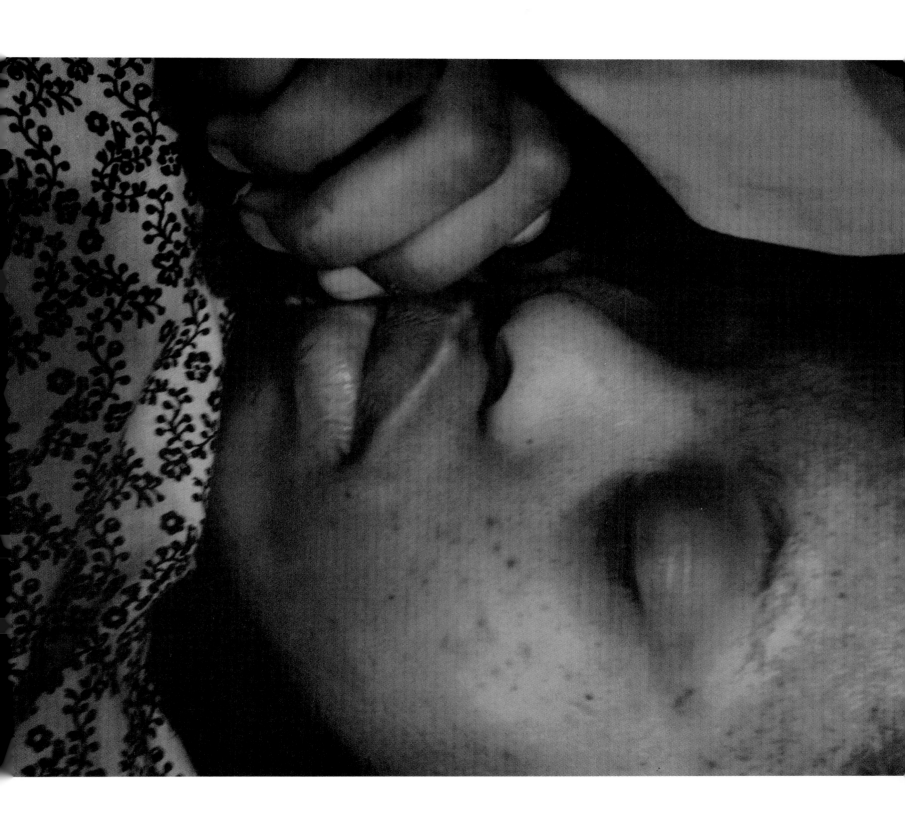

Outside it, the lawn is a carpet and there is a brown tea stain at the centre which must be cleaned but there is no time. There are people building a wall and I know them, two of them, Harrison and Nagy, I haven't seen them in fifteen, twenty years. They know each other but I know they have never met. Haven't we built this wall before, the three of us? My brick is light. When I try to split it, it crumbles. Now there is a crowd around, jostling and pushing because Harrison is fondling a woman's breast. I want to get closer, even though I know this is not real. Let me through, I must get through. People are eating. Fish, but it's raw and whole, not even gutted and what I want is not here, it's there on that bridge across the canal, hundreds of miles away.

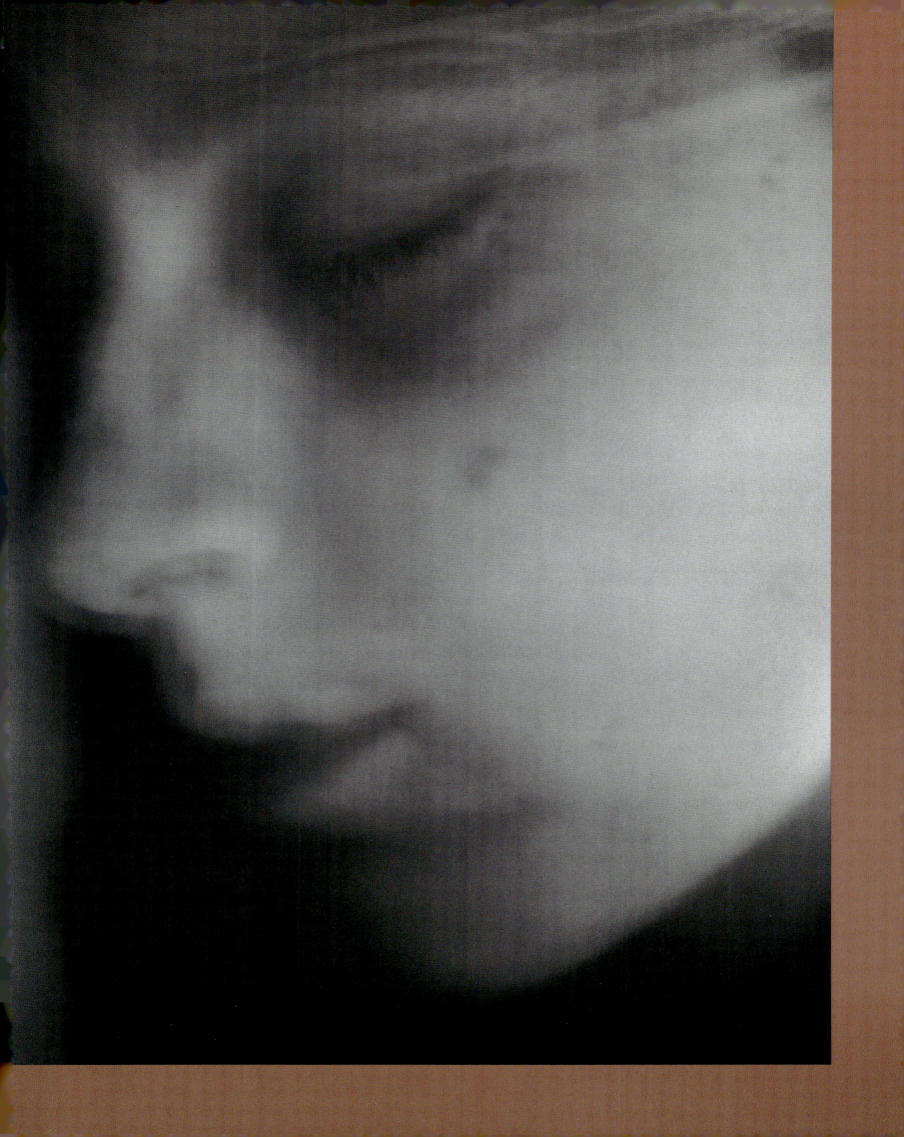

(1) Think of them as elasticated bags. The more space we can provide around the bags, the more room they will have to stretch and the more we can push into them.

(2) To provide that space we need to use the diaphragm and the intercostal muscles. The diaphragm is a sheet of muscle attached to the lower ribs and to the lumbar vertebrae. It rises in the centre to form a dome. Contract this muscle now, pulling the central tendon down: the aim is to enlarge the space in the thorax, the chest cavity. This can only be done at the expense of space in the abdominal organ.

(3) At the same time, contract the intercostal muscles. These span the gaps between the ribs. In contracting them, the chest area becomes deeper as the front of the ribs are raised and wider as the ribs are splayed.

(4) When you successfully operate the diaphragm and the intercostal muscles together, and the thorax is enlarged, atmospheric pressure will force air into the extra space provided. Air may be introduced through the mouth, the nose, or both.

(5) Sitting still, you should aim to process approximately 3.75 litres of air in a minute. This contains 750cc of oxygen, of which you will need to use about a third – 250cc. You do not need to worry about getting the oxygen into the blood system, but you do need to be aware that a transfer takes place: as oxygen enters the blood, it is swapped for carbon dioxide, a waste product that needs to be expelled. This is done by relaxing the diaphragm and the intercostal muscles immediately after you have contracted them. As they are relaxed the chest will return quickly to its unexpanded size and this contraction will in turn enable you to expel carbon dioxide. Again, you may expel through the mouth, the nose, or both.

ATTENTION

All of this needs to happen in the space of a second or two, no more, and should be repeated regularly and indefinitely. The rate of operation will need to be adjusted according to the tasks that you hope to accomplish. You will want to speed up considerably in times of stress.

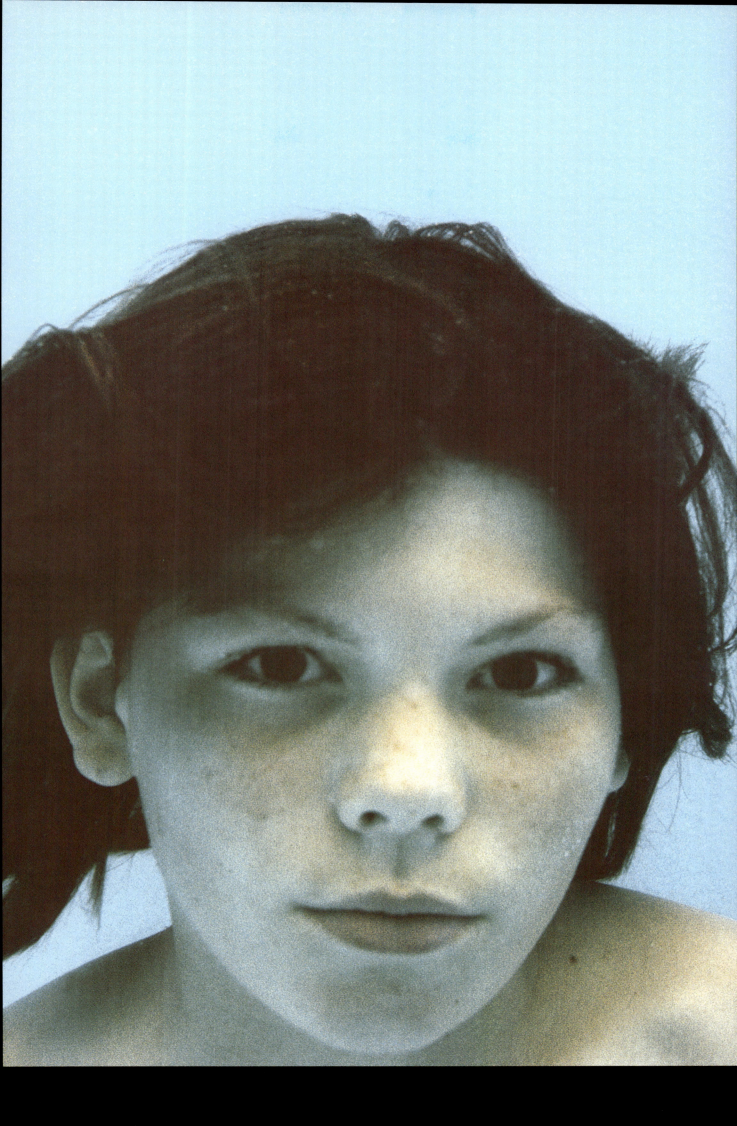

Terry? Chris. How's tricks?

....

Look, you should have called earlier. What number you on anyway?

....

Yeah, and what's your mobile?

....

I can't write it now, I'm on Piccadilly...

....

No, I'm walking, couple of things to take care of. Call back and leave it on the message service.
If you tap in star-one-three-nine after you've spoken you can check if it's taped it OK. Where are you going to be later?

....

I'll be on this one till four, if you can't get me then - bugger.

....

No, not you –

....

Then call me on Linda's, you've got her number, it's on the answer machine message.

....

Listen you're cracking up a bit, do you want to say that again?

....

No, I didn't see it, any good?

....
Well then, they deserved it.
....
....
....
Hold it – sausage and mustard on brown not granary and a tea three sugars to go. And give me a couple of Kit Kats.
....
I'm here. Listen, tell him he can get me on this one whenever.
....
....
Just a sec, just a sec, I've got to get the pager... She can wait. Go on.
....
The point is, it's about being there and being available, whenever, whatever, and that's what they don't seem to twig. Where are you now anyway?
....
And what time do you reckon you'll be there?
....
....
....
....
I've got to go. Check in later, there's some stuff I need to tell you. You know how to get me.

2pm - Northcott Mouth, Cornwall

2am - Trafalgar Square, London

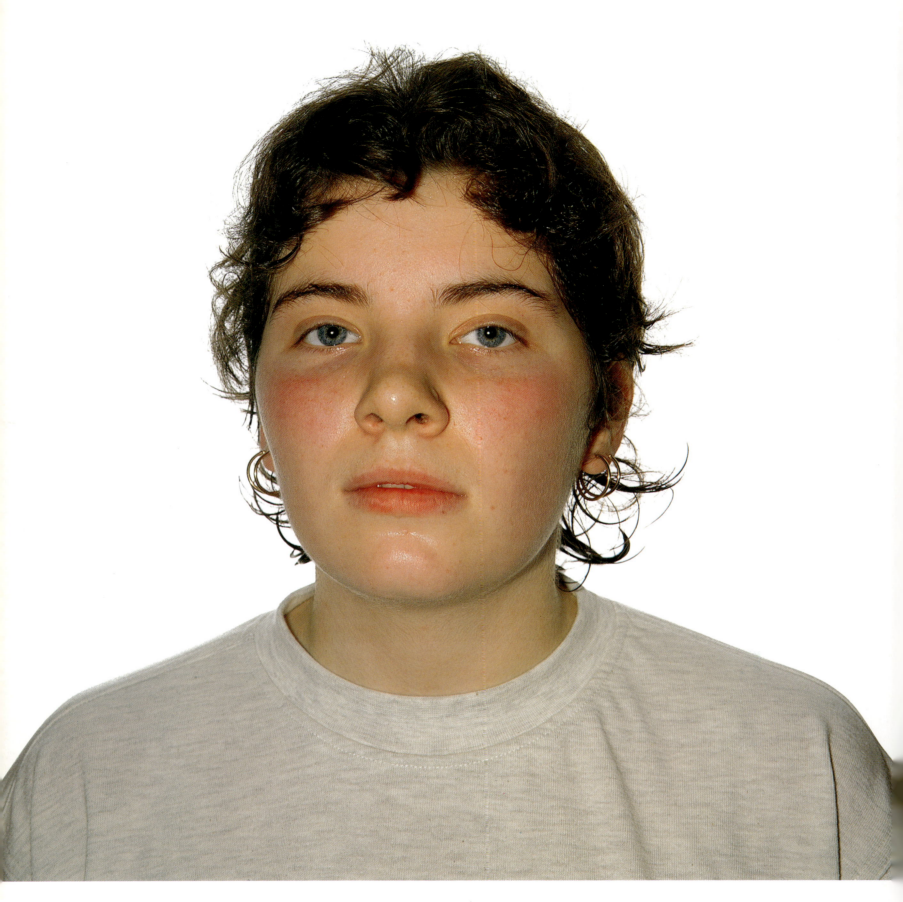

Lunch time - Womens' gym, London

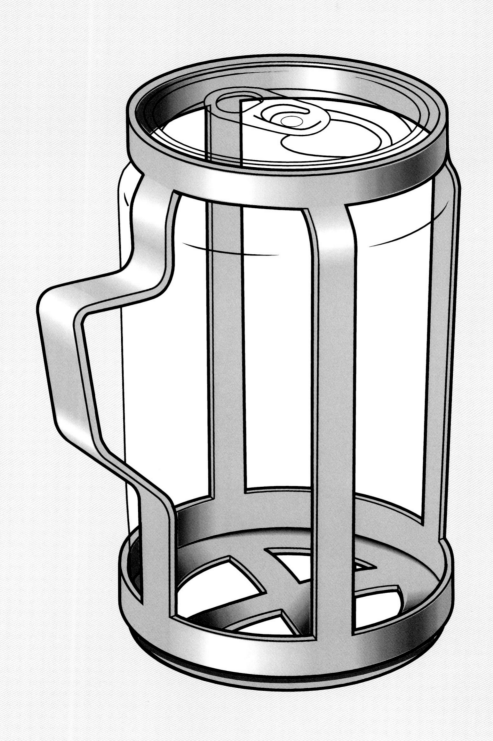

Cash.

It's heavy, it's dirty, you don't want it in your life.

So use the five-pound cash card. For cigarettes, a magazine, a pint of milk. For when signing takes too long and cash is too much trouble. It's a cleaner way of doing business. You're busy, you're stretched but you want goods up to the value of £5. Take them to the till, get your cash card laser-scanned and you're on your way. Buy as many £5 units as you want. We'll keep adding them to your card. And any change you're owed from transactions of less than £5, we'll automatically add to your balance.

The Five Pound Card.
Use it tomorrow. Because life's too short for change.

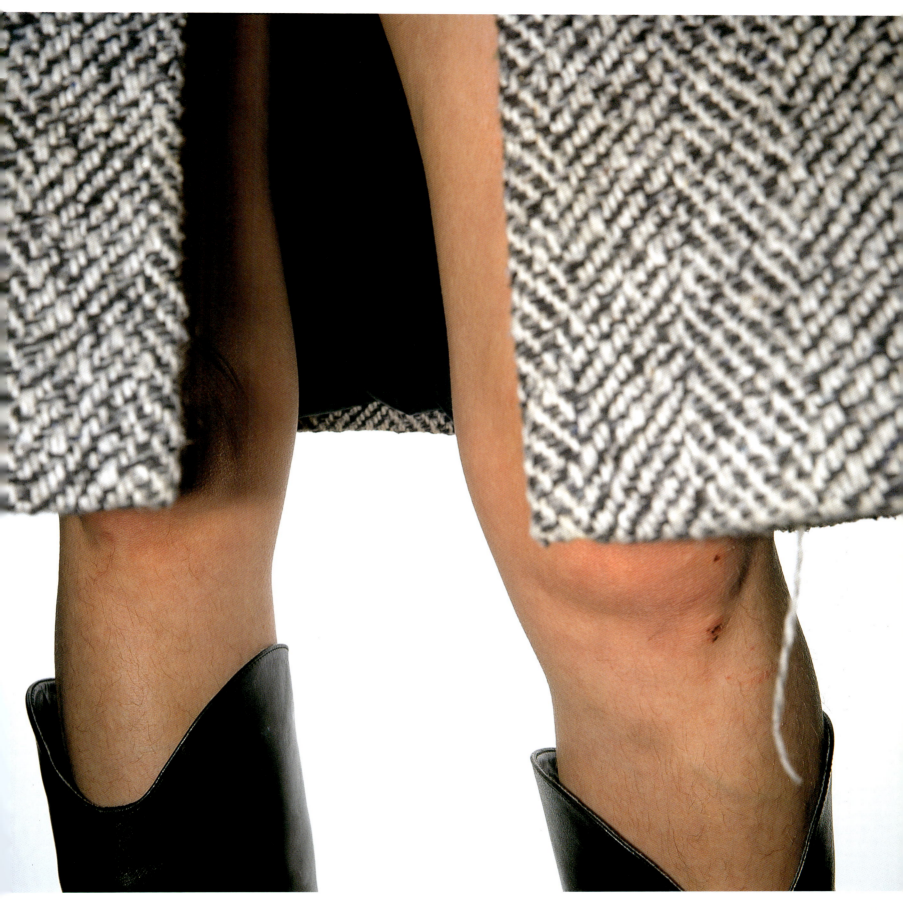

11pm - Commercial Street, London

Chapter 2

Leisure

Prevent Contact With Eyes

It's like nothing else I know. It totally takes you over – you know, you live it and breathe it. I started at fifteen – sixteen years ago when I was a kid. Of course you know nothing then, make a lot of stupid mistakes, but it's the only way to learn. It's like everything else, you start at the bottom, pick up a little bit here, a bit more there, listen to people, watch, read the literature. I started with a tank, gravel, cold water, a couple of plants and an ornamental diver. Plastic. Right now I'm running two tanks. A 4 by 3 by 2 which is basically Discus – that's a South American cichlid, compressed body, bright colour. You're either Discus or you're not. There are some real Discus nuts around. The other's a 5 by 2 by 2 marine tank with undergravel and twin power-head filtration, a protein skimmer and internal carbon filtration. There's a mixture of fish and invertebrates in there, and I want to add on a wave simulator to run on two pow-erheads. Tanks really reflect their owners. You know, someone who likes luxury and sophistication is going to have Dwarf Gouramis and Angels, someone who's maybe more down to earth and outgoing will have Cardinal Tetras, Rams, and brightly coloured gravel. And you can tell a lot about people from the kind of lights they have – Tritons? Sunglos? Lifeglos? Floraglos? Combinations? Obviously, the dream is a reef tank and the secretary of our Aquarist Society knows everything about them and has been steering me towards one for some time. We call him Keef the Reef, for obvious reasons. But it's a hell of a job. You need a shed-load of gear to keep it alive and run-ning. Your filter's got to be able to handle the ammonia and nitrate levels, you need to set it up with Flex-Rings in the trickle tower and Siporax in the sump underneath. The live rock alone is about £150 and that's before you've even thought about the fish.

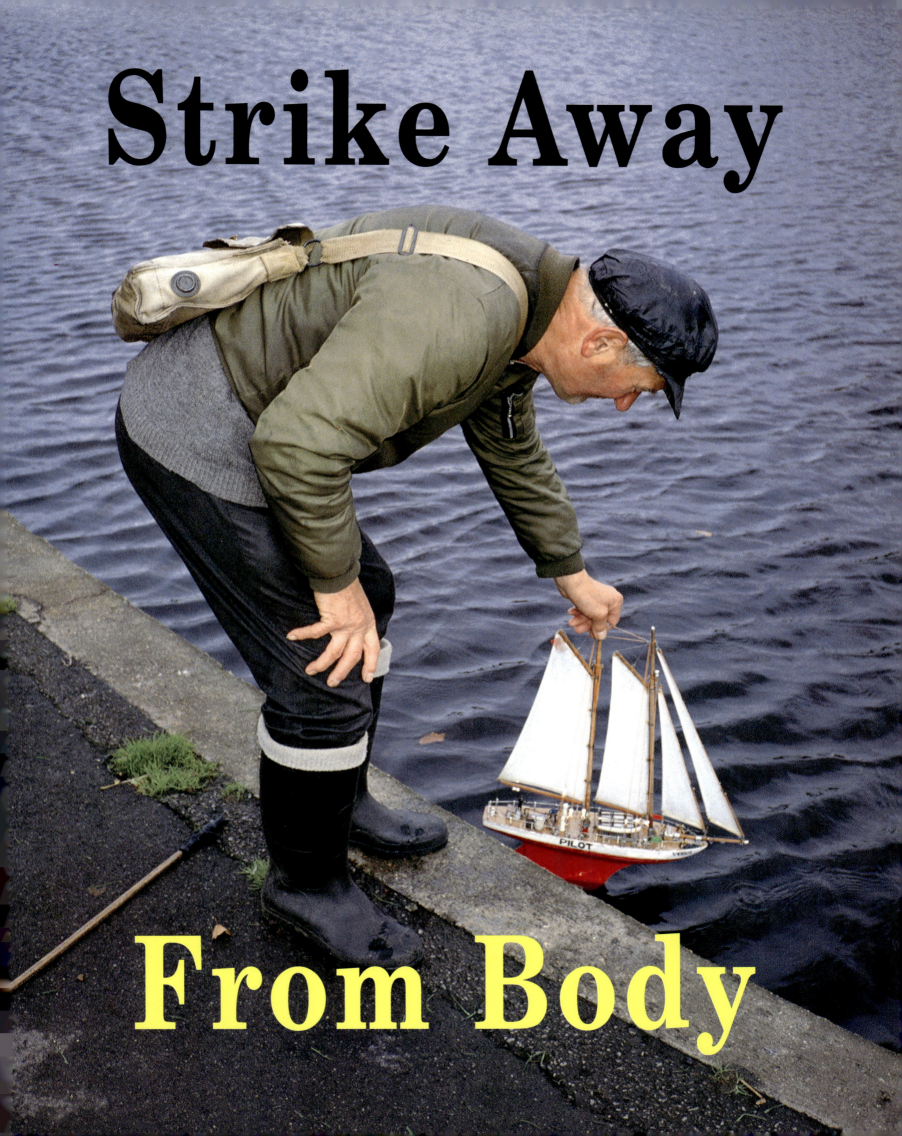

Avoid

Exposure To Danger

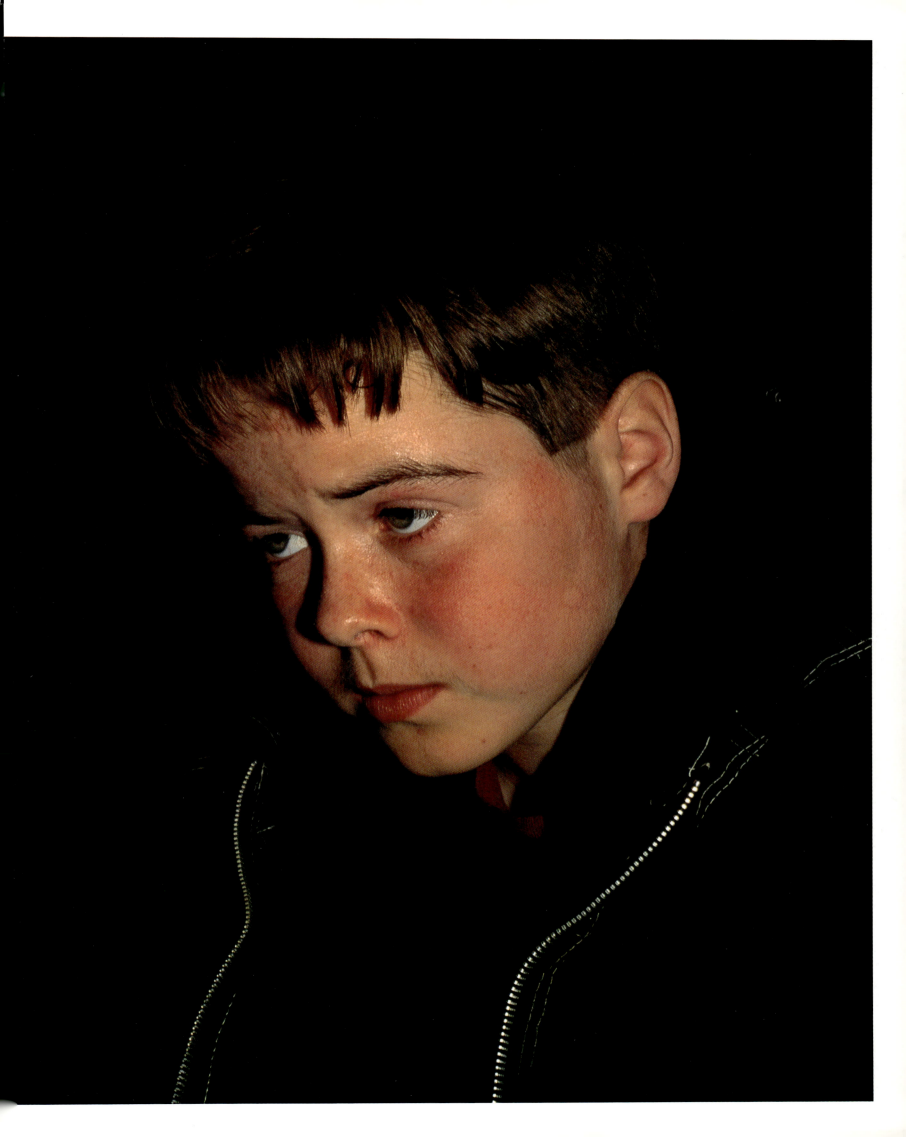

Strapped to a shining slab, white light in her eyes, Anna Kantor could not have known where she was. Quicksilver figures of indeterminate shape darted about at the edge of her vision. A low wailing filled her ears. Then an image appeared, sharp and bright in front of her.

'What is this?'

What she saw were untidily cut discs laid out on a black background. They had a shell-like pattern on them and a crumbly texture.

'Quick! Tell me now!'
'They are... they are biscuits. Cookies... um, from Italy, or France.'

The wailing rose in pitch and volume. Anna realised she was being laughed at.

'No! Wrong! They are foraminifera, single-celled organisms whose fossilised shells are preserved in the sediment on ocean floors... What is this?'

Now she saw a flush of red and scarlet and wine, riven with tiny lines and dark patches.

'This is... this is not blood,' said Anna, her confidence growing. 'This is a heat-sensitive satellite image of a desert, the Gobi or the Sahara maybe, and the dark patches are dunes and the lines are water, deep beneath the surface.'
'Ha! Wrong, wrong, wrong. It is the lower left corner of the robe of St Jerome from the altar painting of the Madonna and saints by Giovanni Bellini in the church of San Zaccaria in Venice. Your last question!'

Up flashed a pale, blotchy landscape of lines, patterned as if cut by a plough and slashed across with deeper, meandering furrows. Anna stared at its contours, crevices and ridges, straining to imagine herself walking through them.

'It is something small, not large,' she said slowly.
'Hurry,' came the voice. 'Last chance!'
'It is the wing of something tiny. The wing of a fly.'
'No! Ha, ha! It is the palm of your left hand!... Take her away.'

Heroes worship.

1   Each player shall have a bat.

2   The playing field shall be free of obstructions.

3   Using the bat in as skilful and ingenious a manner as possible, each player shall aim to hit the puck past his opponent's bat, thus scoring a 'point'.

4   The score shall be displayed at the top of the playing field.

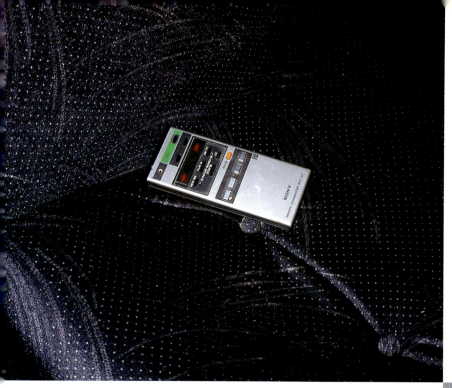

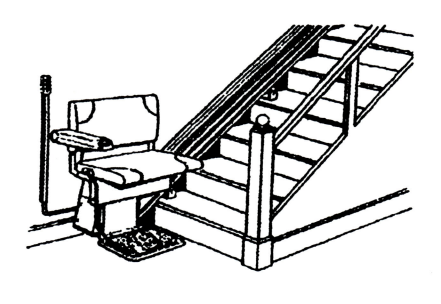

Leisure is the world's largest industry.

Chapter 3

Chaos

Cross-that-troubled-bridge-when-I-get-to-it, on a scale of one to five how tired? One and a half. Good. Seven and three quarter hours' sleep, not drunk, and dreamt... dreamt that I could hover just above the river and swim a very fast crawl without touching the water, and then breast-stroked into a crowded room where the blonde mother-of-a-small-child from upstairs whose name is Tina was... about to get on a train somewhere. Pakistan. Sunshine. Open a window. Cool air feels good around the ear. Small itch upper left leg. Cash? Mm. Keys. And no odd hairs around the chin. Takes the bend one-handed, could do it with one finger, a fingernail even.

'And the question at 8.17 is, why did the chicken cross the road? Gary, it had to be to avoid exits 2 and 3 gyratory this side of the B7863 until at least the middle of next week, also Thatchett Lane – not nice at all.'

Hatchett? Thatchett? Take a left, miss it. Bugger. Stuck. OK... don't get sweaty, no need, 15, no 17 minutes left.

'Circulatory problems at Wadley Corner are causing delays, lights out reportedly nearby so if you are headed eastwards, for goodness sake try not to.'

Eastwards... sun is above, behind, so this is west, more south-west. Left here, worth a detour to miss it. Keep moving, penalty points if you stop.

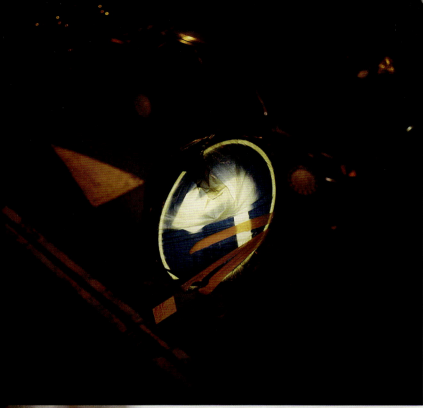

Apparently when Arabs have drivers they tell them just to keep moving, they can't stand stopping.
'Looking good northwards, but south of that it's calamity corner with multiple diversions in operation, and delays of up to an hour.'

Where? Just say where, we won't go there. Right at the end and... shit, back in the middle of it, unless he lets me... bastard. Sweat coming under left arm, one drop running straight down, trapped it where the belt meets the shirt. Just the body's cooling system, without it you'd die in minutes. Do fish sweat? Cheese does. Not when it's runny.

'...and news that the link access slipway has shed its load causing multiple aspersions, consequently standard inversions are in operation there...'

Collision collusion conversion diversion. Hairy Mary, quite contrary. Hot now. Feet are swelling. Need to go now please thank you very much.

'...which means that drivers are warned to expect reduced flow contrariwise until tea time...'

Iced tea. Contrary to what?

'...not normally a problem but today there it's haywire, gridlock while a burst anterior arterial main is severed prior to reconjunction at a later juncture...'

Haylock... Conjunctivitis. Glare. Right palm sweaty. No breeze. Not moving.

'...unconfigured interstices still causing infraction, persistent clumping not likely to ease restrictions...'

Infraction. Infection. Network is infected.

'...undecided intersections causing clamping likely to please constrictions...'

'...reconvened interface switchback by-pass inadvisable resurfaced until middle of Nick's ear reverse operation roundabout overload. That's it.'

INDICATE PURE AREA

LEFT

RIGHT

'The Faction doesn't care what we think, it cares only that we are eliminated.' Frisco looked at Krutek and Whisper. Krutek spoke next, so softly the others could scarcely hear him. 'Then we must strike first. We know what we have to do.' 'But they are hundreds,' Frisco countered, 'and we are three.'

Whisper closed his fist around the aluminium sheet on which the proclamation was inscribed. As he screwed it into a tiny ball his bicep burst through the sleeve of his tunic, revealing the scar left by Vantulé's duelling laser.

 'Three grammes of Destructoplasma can raze a six-storey module. A single burst from a laser assault pistol can eliminate twenty men. Friends, we have the power to rip this city apart.'

Frisco reached for his night helmet. All three clenched their fists and stared hard in the direction of the citadel. Outside the compound, women and infants gathered to watch and cheer as the trio of armed avengers strode towards their destiny.

Chapter 4

Spoilt

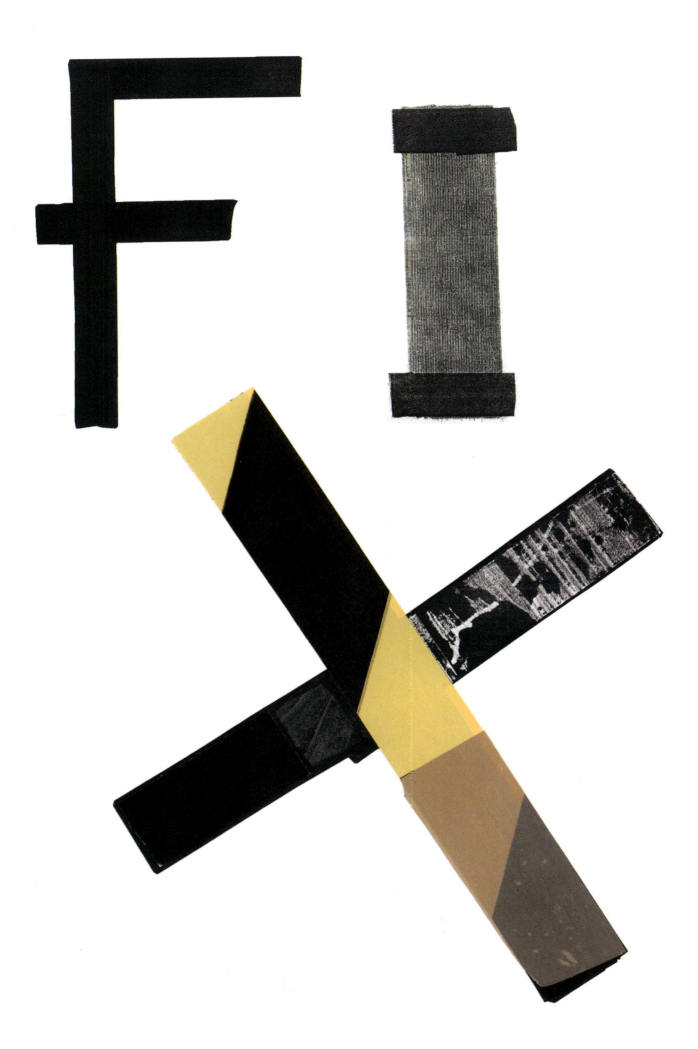

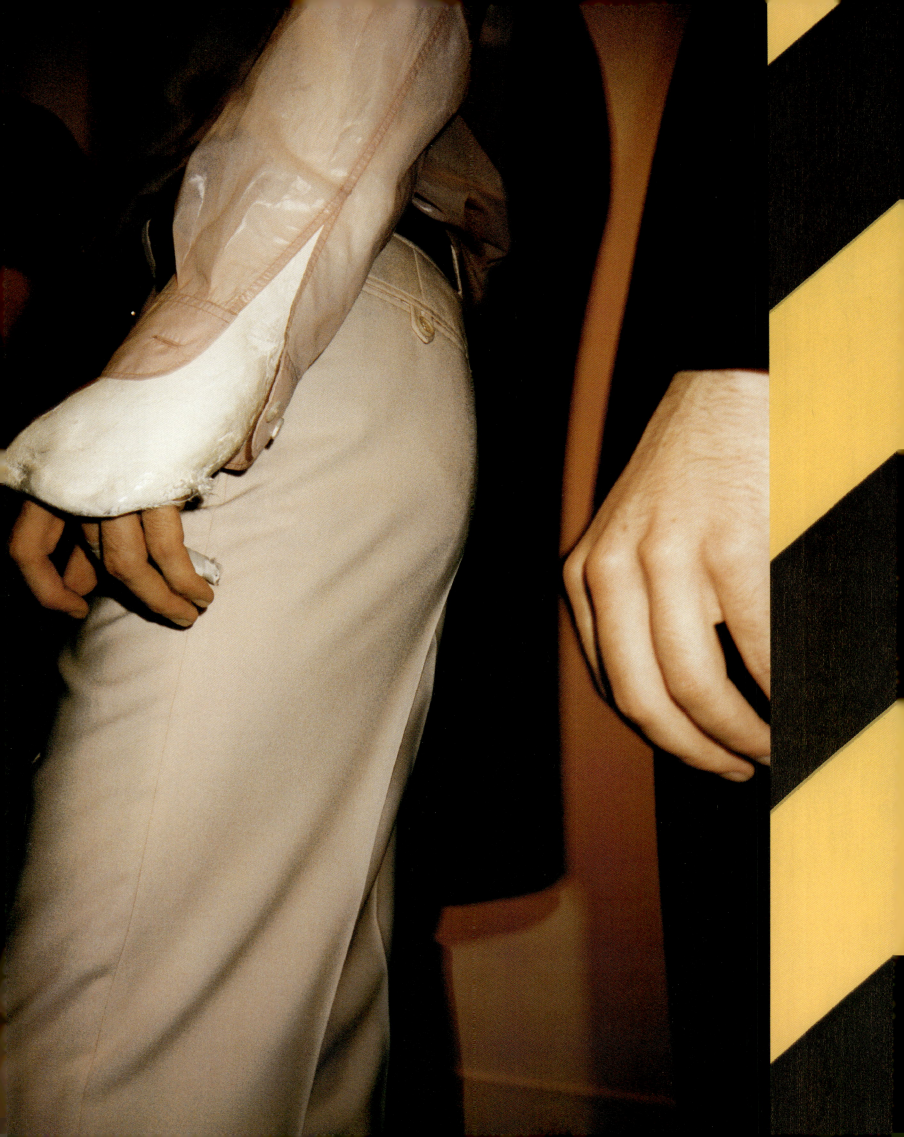

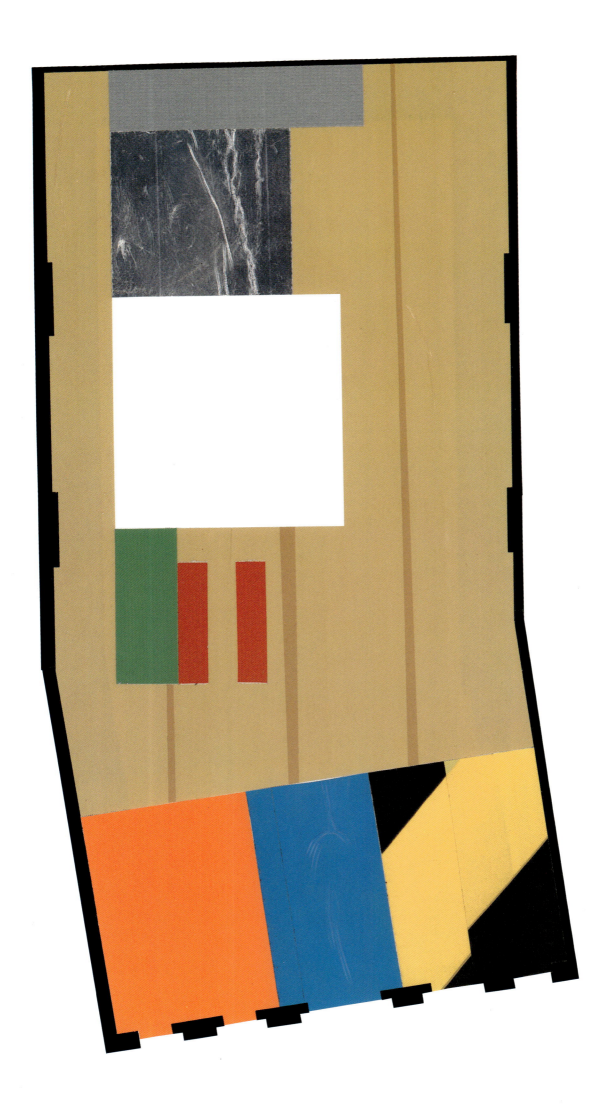

Moving through to the main reception room, the folded postcards are used as wedges to stop the sash windows rattling. It is inadvisable to open the far left window. Should this be unavoidable, the wooden knife block from the kitchen is used to prop it open. Without this, the window may fall sharply causing injury.

This second-floor flat in a converted Victorian terrace has two bedrooms, two reception rooms, period fittings, a fully modernised kitchen and enjoys south-facing views affording copious natural light all year round.

The co-ordinated bathroom has a bidet, bath and power shower. When using the shower it is important not to leave the cold tap in the kitchen running, since this will result in scalding water in the bathroom. After flushing the toilet it is necessary to wiggle the handle quickly two or three times, otherwise the cistern will not fill up.

Bookshelf space is limited: this can be supplemented by using the lower two cupboards in the kitchen, into which standard paperbacks fit comfortably. Also in the kitchen is the washing machine. Due to a wiring problem, the only setting that works is 'cold', though in fact this delivers hot water. For a warm or cool wash, add a glass of cold water manually at the beginning of the programme. Use the paperclip to secure the door of the machine. Placing the iron, the kettle (full) and the bread bin on top will stop the machine moving across the floor during the spin cycle.

In the hallway, you may see a two-pence piece glued to the inside of the lampshade. This acts as a counterweight and should not be removed. If it is necessary to replace the lightbulb, do not stand on the small table. The glue holding the rear right leg in place dried out some years ago and it will now only support the weight of a coat or vase, etc.

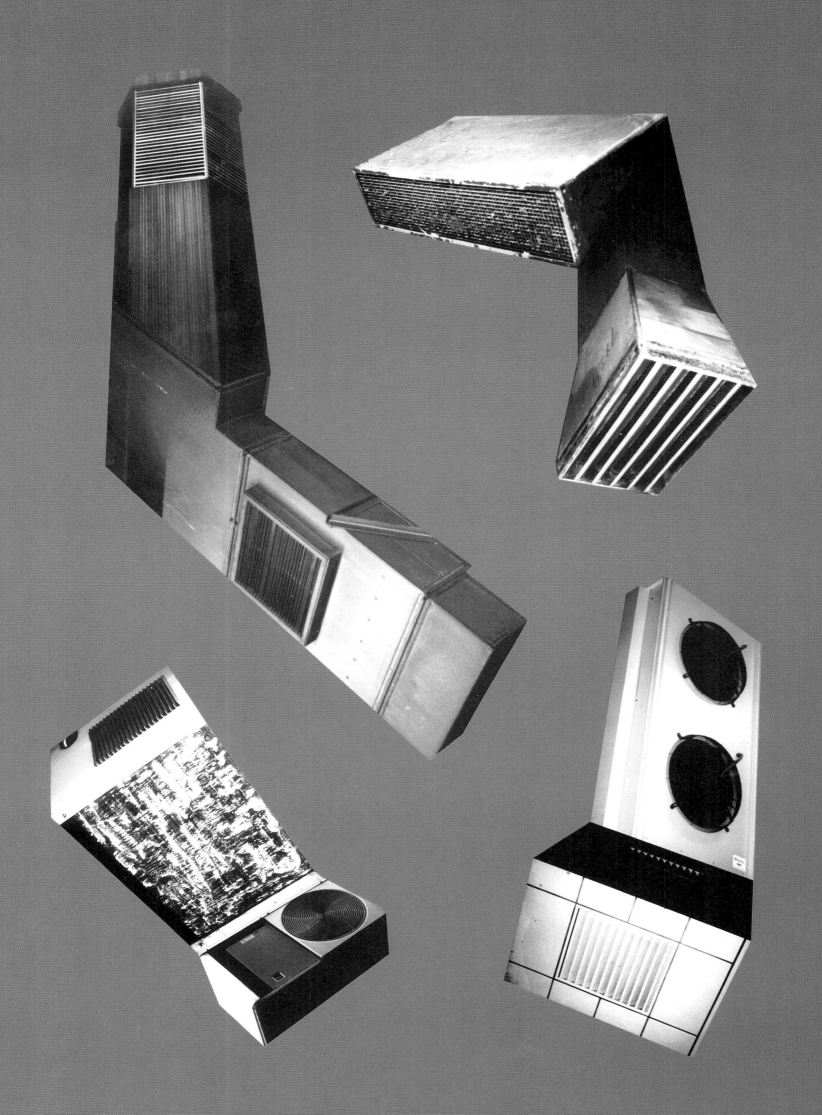

Chapter 5

Aspire

'I had three ambitions when I was a child:
to be a painter, to be a millionaire and to
be a dandy. I've never had a job... Work is
when you get paid for doing what you don't
want to do, isn't it? I get up at 6.30 and run five
miles. I come back at 8.00, read the FT and sit
here at the screen till 10.00. At 11.00 I'm at the
easel, I work until 1pm. I'm in touch with this the
whole time. It's programmed to beep if things move.
I stop for lunch, then I go back to the easel from 3.00
till 5.00 At 5.00 I stop, and in the evening I go out to
supper with friends. That's all I do. Making money is an
art not a science. You find people buy paintings in the
same way that people buy stocks and shares. Jeff Koons
was a stockbroker and you can see that in his art. Cézanne
was also a stockbroker and Gauguin, too. There are no ethics
or morality in business, but the artists I know are not ethical
or moral either. Art is dissident isn't it? You can't think about
morality when you paint and you can't when you do this. I mean,
I ought to sell Shell oughtn't I? They're very naughty, aren't
they, in Nigeria? The market works on fear and greed. It's gambling, don't let anyone tell you it isn't. It's an addiction. I'm
addicted and I'm also addicted to painting. In both you risk
complete failure. You do as a painter or you're not alive.
I think it was Nietzsche who said to live fully you need
to live dangerously. You only know you're an animal
that dies if you touch death with your lips. Painting
makes me feel alive and gambling makes me feel
alive. I've got a strong urge to self-destruct, my
work's all about death. It's the same with this, I
could self-destruct. I take very big risks. I want
to be really rich, I want to have millions. If I really took off as a painter I wouldn't give this up.
Money is good, it isolates you from the hard-
ships in life. It's very expensive being rich
as well, so you need as much as you can get.'

PURSU
IT OF
EXCEL
LENCE

Listen closely and you will hear the ocean roar.

Look up beyond the light and see the moon.

You are shedding all that slows you, all that holds you back.

Embrace yourself, love yourself, feel yourself soar.

Feel your breathing, feel the power within you.

There is a force you possess that is

stronger than gravity.

Let it lift you up above the world.

There is nothing you cannot conquer,

no one you need fear.

When you enter a room, fill it.

When you leave, it will be smaller.

When the time comes for closure,

hit hard and hit fast.

When you meet an obstacle,

do not change course -

think of the athlete and hurdle it.

You are walking above the ground,

floating on the cushion of your talent.

And now you are ready.

Recognise your enemy.
There is no margin for error.

RRRR ERROR

2 3 4 5 6 7 8

EVERY IDEOLOGYIS AREFL ECTIO NOFEC ONOMI CCIRC UMSTA NCE.

Chapter 6

Product

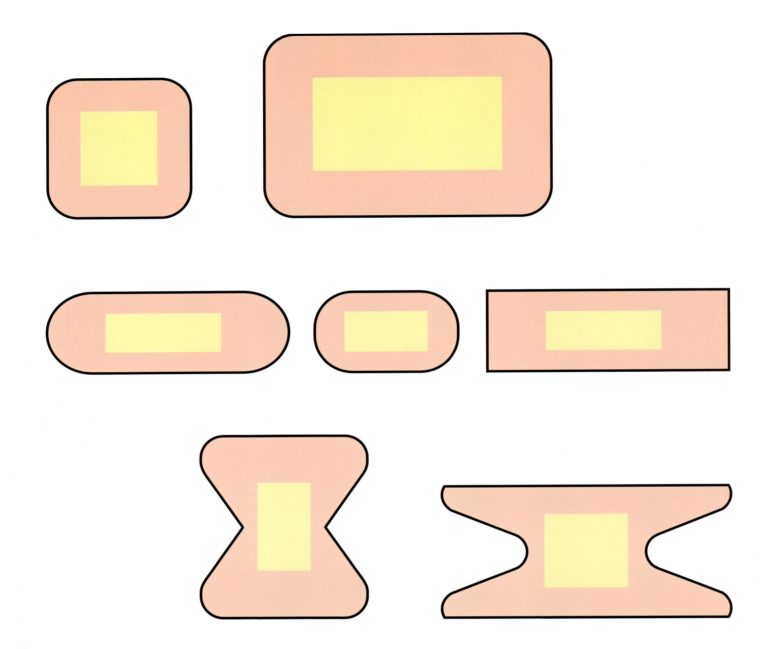

Original

Copy

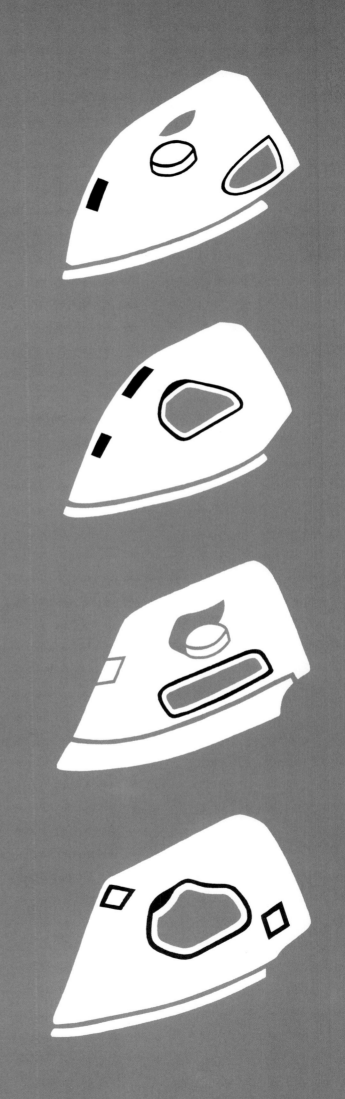

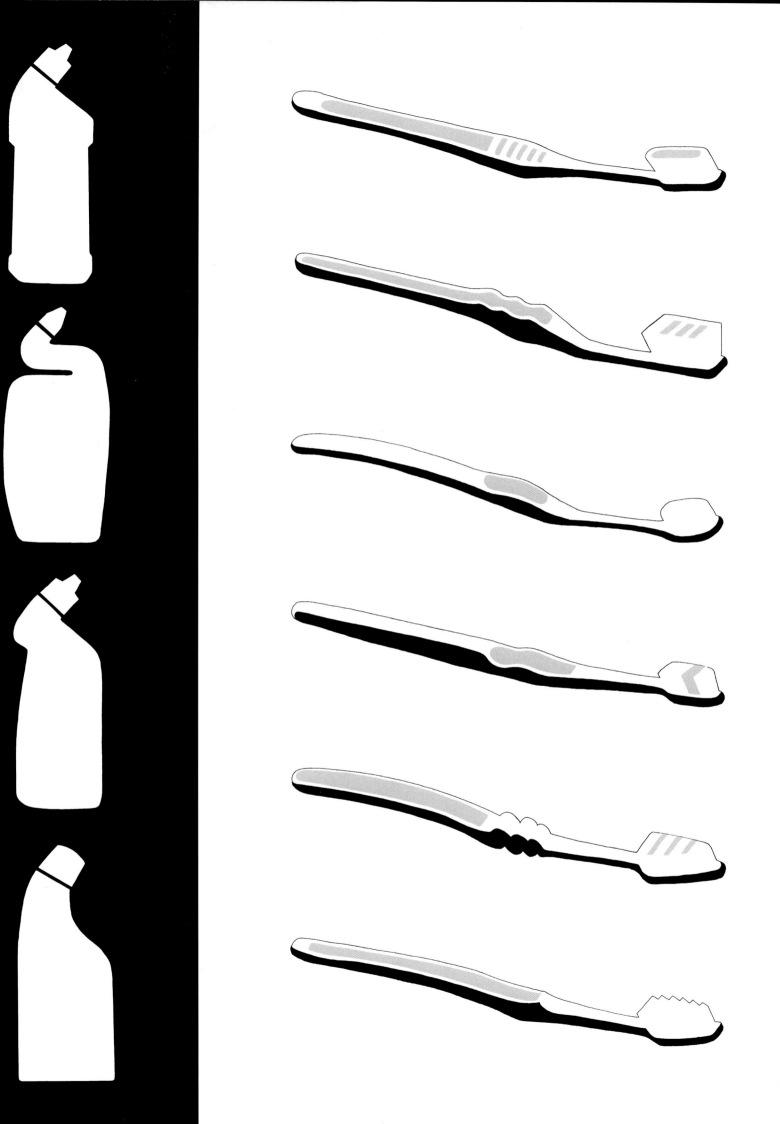

Pure product is a product with no application.

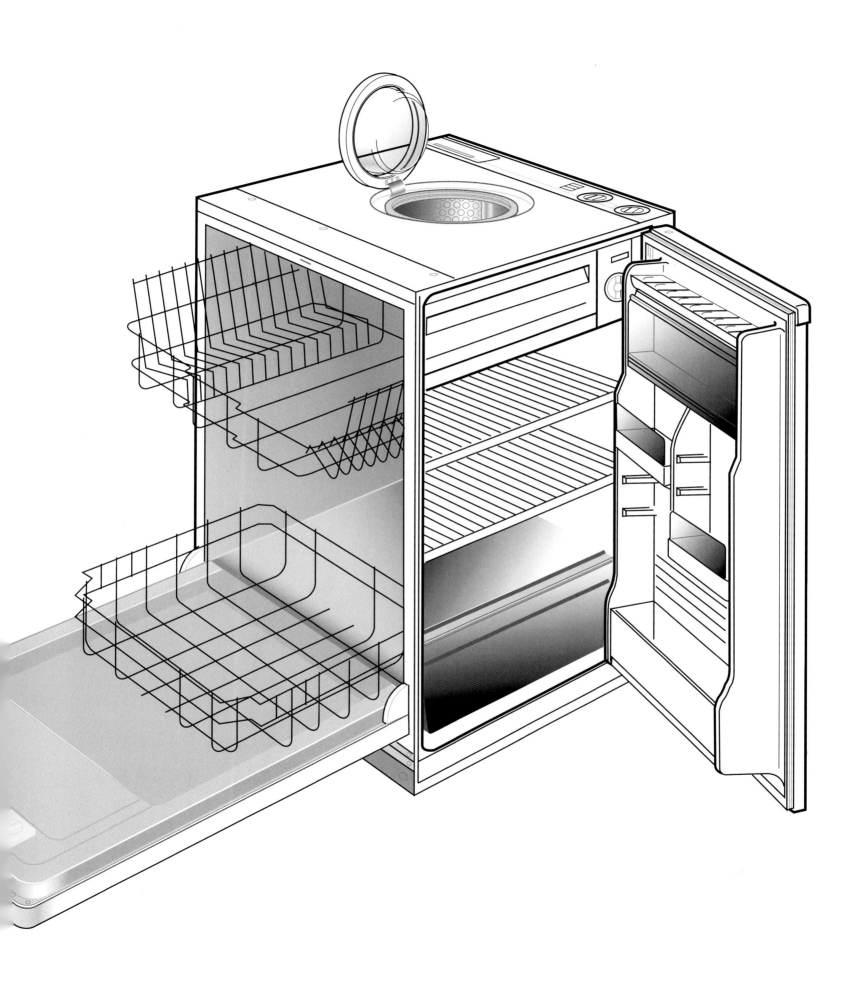

The Pure

products

of

America

go

crazy.

Chapter 7

Bred

And often, too, the beginnings went unnoticed
As though the story could advance its pawns
More discreetly thus, over stepping
The confines of ordinary health and reason
To introduce in another way
Its fact into the picture.

John Ashbery

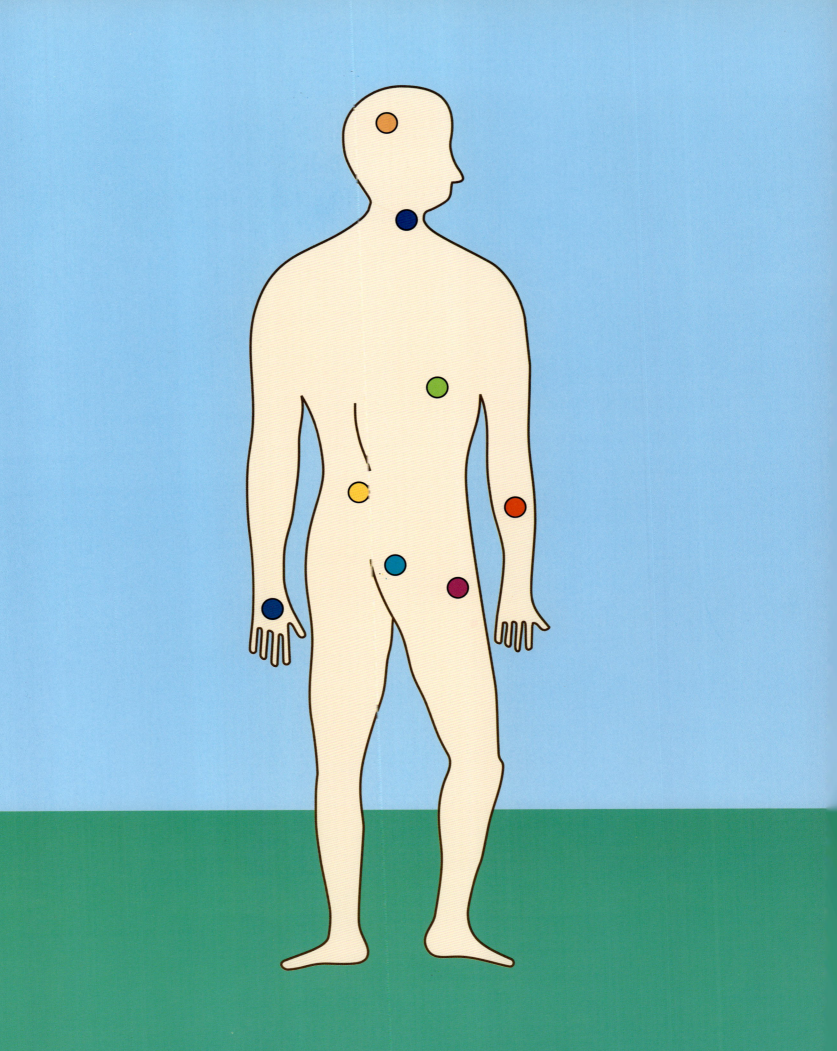

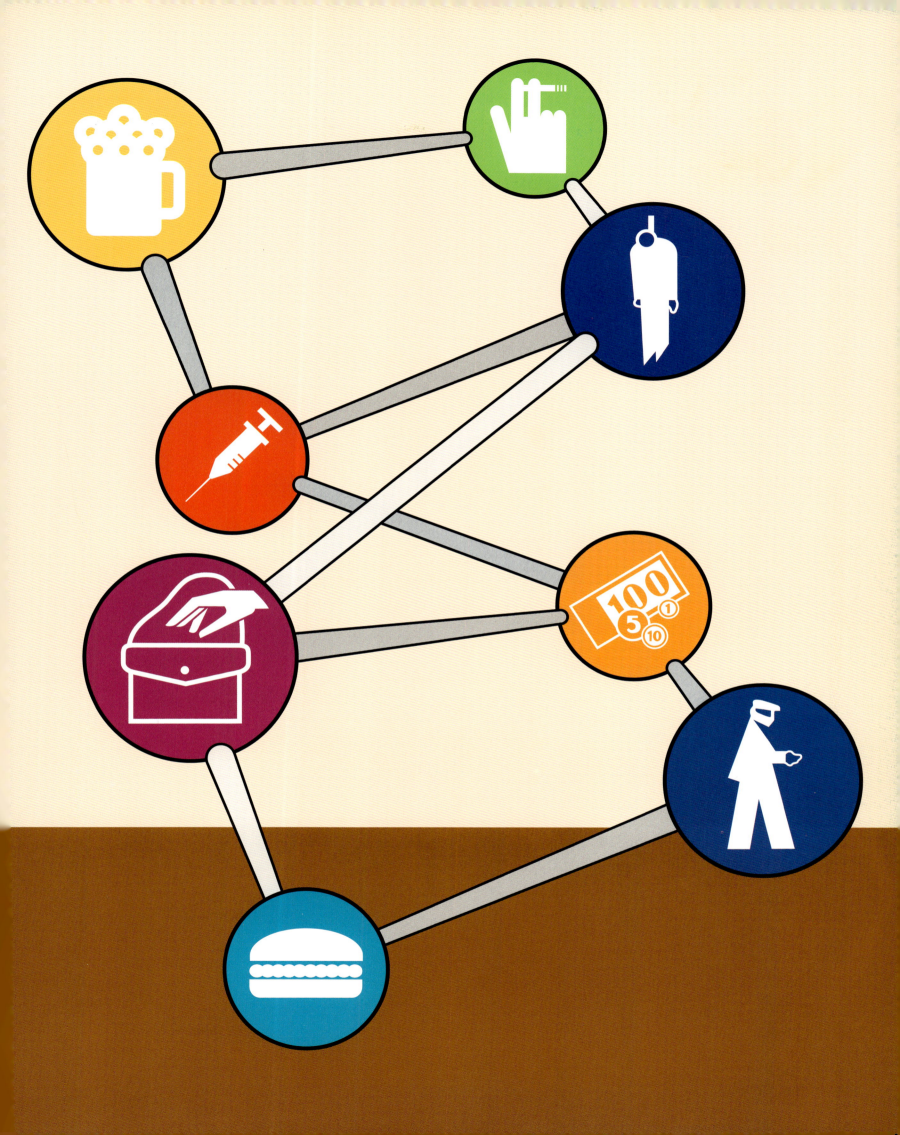

Trust, Donate. Do All That Is Asked.

SPREAD
THE VIRUS

And He
Shall Give
You Rest.

When Audrey Hunter discovered that the Universe was composed mostly of dust she did not, unlike others who heard the news, pause in wonder but picked up a cloth, pulled the sofa away from the wall and cleaned the length of skirting board she had been meaning to for the last six months.

Had he been home that day, Reginald Hunter would, no doubt, have helped her, since theirs was a marriage characterised by co-operation, affection in adversity and unshifting attention to domestic detail.

They met, as Reginald was to tell the policeman, 36 years before Audrey's eventual demise. She lived in comfort with her widowed mother in Clapham – a small terraced house left to them by her father, a travelling salesman (dead, too young, of emphysema). Audrey, who no one thought pretty, married the first man she danced with: Reginald Hunter of Battersea, an undertaker's assistant with plans, who parted and Brylcreem'd his hair in a manner that was a little passé even in 1956, but which her mother took as a sign of earnestness suggesting that he might make a steady income, if not better.

Audrey never worked, unless you call cooking and cleaning and two years as a dental receptionist 'work', which she didn't. Reginald went to night school and took his qualifications to an accountancy firm, which hired him on the spot. He rose, not far, but far enough to take Audrey from a basement flat in Clapham (close to mother), to a mansion flat in Herne Hill and, at last, to a semi-detached house in Merton with a gate, a garden, a garage and gravel on the drive.

They had no children – she couldn't – so they made the best of a nephew and two nieces, friends and each other. Their photograph albums were full; they holidayed in Cornwall, the Algarve, Garmisch Partenkirchen and, once, Tunisia. They had a dog for a decade, then they kept fish – tropicals – until one summer the filter gave up, the fish died and they couldn't be bothered with more.

He spoiled her, she said, spending too much every birthday, but the present she loved most was the wedding photograph he mounted, framed and hung on the wall to surprise her, unveiling it with a showman's tug as if it were the inscribed cornerstone of the house, which in a sense it was.

She went suddenly, next to him, in the night. He didn't know when. He woke up to find her hand on his chest. When he lifted it, it was cold. He did what he'd had to do once before for his mother: rang the doctor, then her sister, then an undertaker. People didn't rush round, nor did he want them to. As he put out the rubbish that first morning he wanted to ask her what she'd meant by saying 'That's you to a T', even when he realised that he couldn't, never would, there was still her presence, still the comfort of knowing she was there. The only thing that could disrupt that would be if someone came to take her away.

Geo. Napley & Nephew, the firm he had once worked for, were commissioned to handle the arrangements. Reginald told them he knew it was old fashioned, but he wanted Audrey to lie in the front room before they took her. Frank and Mary thought it strange, but the nieces came to pay their respects and Audrey's sister Susan kissed her on the forehead.

Early that morning while she was being prepared, he went out in the car to Smithfield. He came back with a butchered calf in the boot, which he left in the cool of the garage, next to the fish tank.

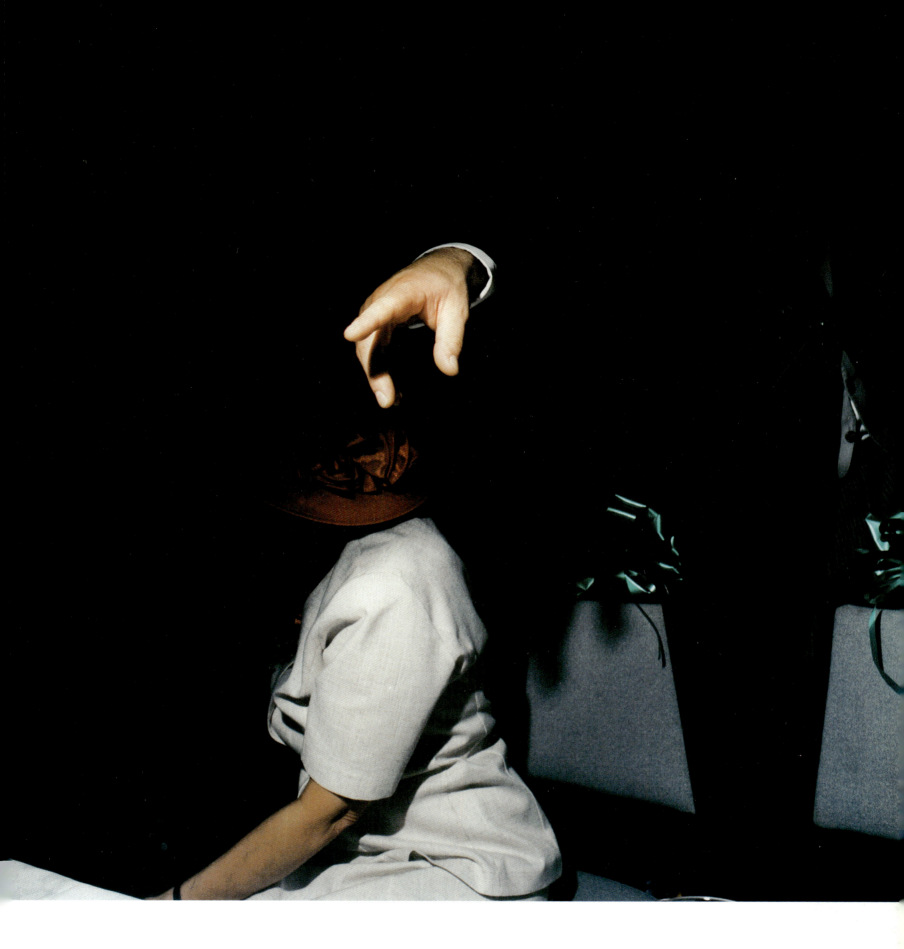

He didn't start out with a plan, more an instinct that something had to be done, though once it became a plan he set about it with absolute concentration. He brought the calf in wrapped in a sack while Susan was making tea in the kitchen, and hid it behind the sofa. When the time came for the funeral everyone knew he wanted two minutes with her alone, so they waited outside on the drive. When Napley's men knocked and came in to carry her away, they found he'd put the lid on by himself. No one thought it odd: it's an old habit, he said, I used to be in the trade myself, I want the job done properly.

After the cremation, people stopped for a drink and were gone. That night, alone again, he dressed her in her favourite woollen skirt and thick Aran cardigan, because he didn't want her to get cold. He brushed her tight little golden curls and picked some fallen hairs from her shoulders. Then he laid her in the fish tank.

Finding the chemicals was easy – he used the Yellow Pages – and so, late the next day, Audrey Hunter, still sleeping, still composed, lying on her side, was sealed in the fish tank.

He did not hide her, he simply moved her to the spare room upstairs which they never used. It became Audrey's room. While being careful not to disturb her privacy, Reginald went in at least once a day thereafter to talk to her. Sometimes he would read to her – something that had caught his eye in the paper or a little poem, sometimes he would just tell her about his day. It became a routine that sustained him. She slept, of course, but what mattered was that she was there.

Three years, two weeks and five days after her death, Paul Kemp came to Wishart Avenue clutching his buckets and a ladder: Paul Kemp, last known address Wormwood Scrubs, but determined to make an honest living, at least until something better came up. He cleaned windows uninvited on the principle that a job well done was something no one could refuse to pay for. And so it was that he lifted his ladder to Audrey Hunter's window, saw a body in a tank and raised the alarm. Reginald was taken to the police station.

Was he 'A weirdo from the start, no question' (Jackie Carter at number 84)? 'A very sad old man' (DC Colin Greening)? He could not say, he did not feel qualified. All he knew was that he had loved her, and now she was gone.

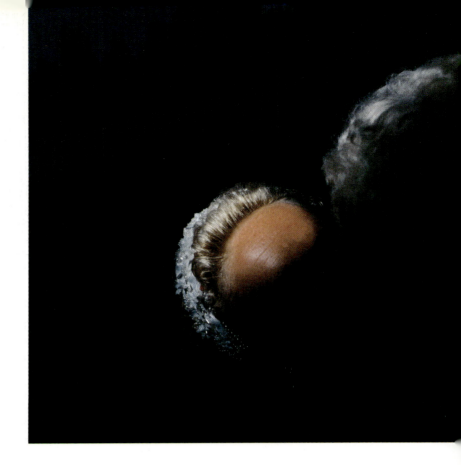

Chapter 8

Society

Welcome to a global society
NOW OPEN

In search of photo opportunity
QUEUE HERE

Addicted consumers of wealth
FREE ENTRY

'My name is Hubert de Villiers. I am capable, constant, rarely mendacious and my skills lie in the areas of interpersonal relations and excavating opportunities from lost causes. I can indeed perform multiplication and additionally subtraction but division is my favourite.

'What have I done today? Today as in the first day of the rest of the best days of our lives? Today I organised my affairs. A complete reappraisal from head to toe of all matters outstanding in all my spheres of concern. I have instigated a three-tier system of staging now which classifies matters for my attention into a) impending b) inconsequential c) derisory. I find that it's speeding things up quite noticeably.

'Today is Tuesday, though it may well be Friday. Obviously in the context of a normal business day I would have that kind of information to hand. I hope you'll bear with me in this instance. What I really want to talk about is the future and how I fit into it. I have plans extant of the grandest order but they are targets to be met only by a genuine liaison at the cutting edge.

'Number nine, Lefever Road... No, the fact of the matter is that I have not the smallest connection with any address of that place though before I go on the record and perjure myself I would want to run a very quick file check to put my mind at rest.

'The Prime Minister lives at number ten Downing Street. We have not met but in the course of daily business and procedure that is only to be expected. His is a vision that I have assimilated and that in broad measure I can do business with. It is imperative that the infra-structure of transport, health, building, wealth, heritage, portfolios, accommodation, should be managed efficiently for all our sakes and my belief is that this is what is happening.

'The sun rises in the East of course and sets in the polar opposite direction, that is the evidence of my observations, and densely packed cumulo-nimbus is a cloud formation.

'Please can I go now?'

Second waitress   Can I get you guys more coffee?

(She smiles. They ignore her. She takes the hint.)

Cop   Open that envelope, Sandy. It's a sworn affidavit that says I've changed.

Nurse   No more hiding from me? No more phone calls from Denver?

Cop   No more laparotomy and no more lies... That person I was then, the one with the wardrobe and the sick habit? You know, I guess I think I saw him on my way in here... Let's just say he was heading out of town.

Nurse   I dreamt about the three of us last night. About the way you carried Chuck across that stream back last winter, and about the baptism, and about what Momma said before she went.

Cop   But that was before the shooting. It was good, and then it was bad, and now it can be good again. Sandy, if you're there pulling with me, I know I can be a detective and a disciple to make you proud.

Nurse   There's someone I think you should meet... CJ, honey... you can come in now. It's time you got to know your father.

Carol and Richard Freeman are now married with three children.

John Mahoney has become a Superior Court Judge in Orange County, California.

Wyn Hamilton attempted to claim the $31,000 reward after the death of Officer Webb.

Her request was denied.

Robert Bruce is serving a life sentence in an Arizona State Penitentiary for being an accessory to two murders.

William Freeman is serving life without the possibility of parole in Folsom Prison.

158

The average Russian lives without war and extreme drinking. He does not kill nor does he bathe in ice cold rivers. He cannot afford goods imported from the West, he has to struggle for a living but is not a beggar. As the outside world is cold and harsh, women make their homes cosy with what is available. During the long, cold winters Russians study astrology, knit pullovers, read Pushkin. Till late at night they sit around the kitchen table talking, philosophising, singing, crying. A guest is holy, he has to eat and drink well, everything that is in the house is put on the table. A Russian is proud, he will stand for hours in the cold, waiting for a bus without complaining; when you bring him a present he will not open it while you are there and afterwards he will say he does not need it. The next day he will give you a present in return. He is easily hurt and shows his anger loudly, but when you become friends with a Russian it is for life.

Chapter 9

Truth

INTE
FR
CRE
O
YO
MONEY

REST EE DIT R UR BACK

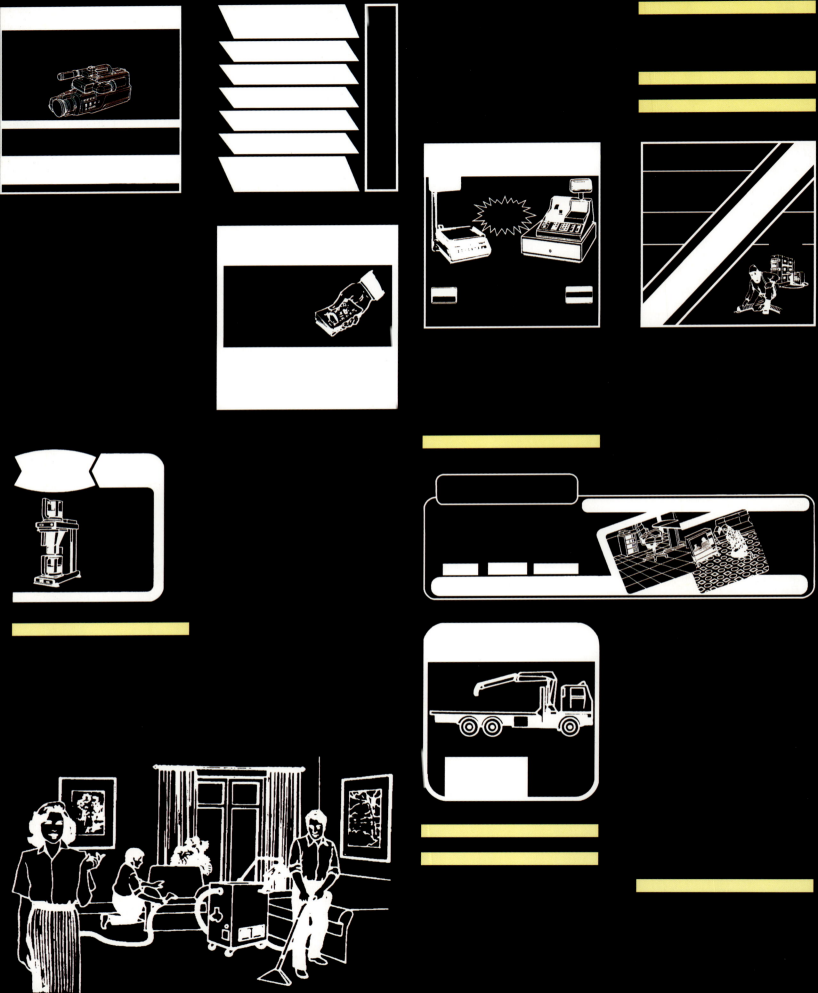

You have a choice. You will be sent to one of two islands. To look at, they are much the same. Green hills, fertile land, clear water: subsistence is not the issue.

There are people on both. Their temperaments are identical. We know nothing of their morals, but they are not savages. Within each island, they live in harmony; their intentions are peaceful, though if necessary they will kill to protect that peace.

The difference between them is this. On the first island, you will be understood only if your diction is precise. You will be judged solely by the meaning of your words. There is no such thing as rhetoric; no one will know the meaning of a nod, a wink or a sly grin. The beseeching wail does not register, nor does the laugh. There will be no ambiguity.

On the second island, the words you use will scarcely matter. Tone of voice, inflection, posture are all the islanders understand. It will not be what you say that counts but how you say it; the gestures that accompany a request, a denial or an admission; the involuntary expressions you assume in silence. You will see that you will have no control over much of what you display.

These are the rules. Whether you choose the first or the second island, you will be met with the same question: do you mean to do us harm? Don't think of it as pleading for your life. All they want to know is the truth.

Real Fruit Flavourings

Chapter 10

Space

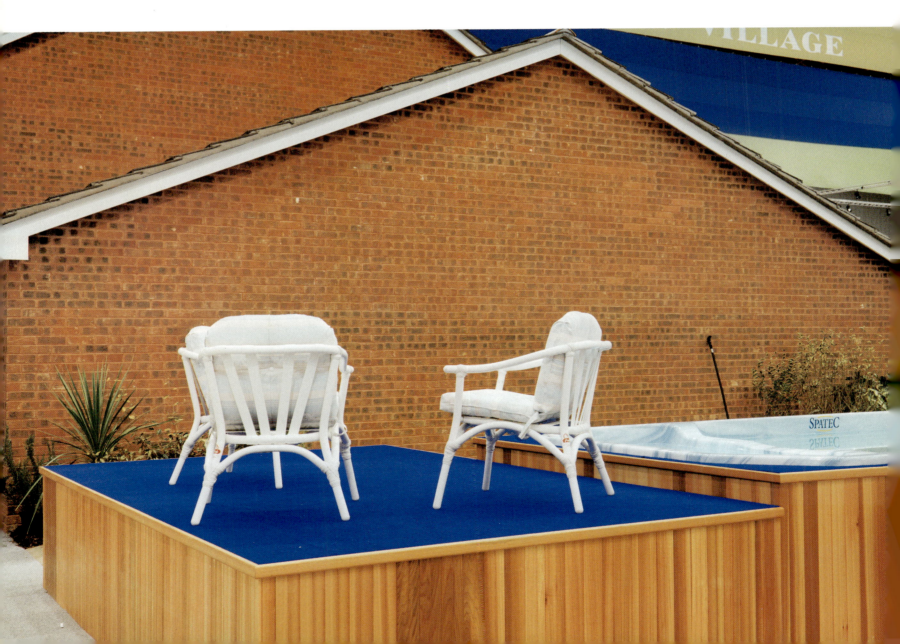

ALL APPOINTMENTS MUST BE
IN WRITING, GIVING 7-
DAYS TIME TO BE CHECK
AND VETTED BY PHONE NO.
NO PLANNED MUGGERS CALLS

WE ARE ALERT
OF THE CRIME PLOTS
NEIGHBOURHOOD
WATCH
CRIME PLOTTERS
WARNING

SAFTY FIRST, IF IN
DOUBT, KEEP ALL
CALLERS OUT.
I WAS MUGGED
RIGHT HERE.

Phone Police. 999

POLICE
999 emergency

Watch
out!
There's a thief
ab•ut

CRIME
NEIGHBOURHOOD
WATCH
You're
already well
equipped to prevent
crime.
BE ALERT
DIAL 999
AND CALL POLICE

NO

THANK YOU

A WISE PERSON ARMED
ONE SELF. BECAUSE A
FOOL MAY ATTACK YOU
AT ANY TIME. ALWAYS BE
ON YOUR GUARD. AND BE
PREPARE FOR ATTACK.

BEWARE
Danger Electricity

PLEASE KEEP OU

MINIMUM LIVING REQUIREMENTS
Height : 7ft 6 Width : 8ft Length : 10ft

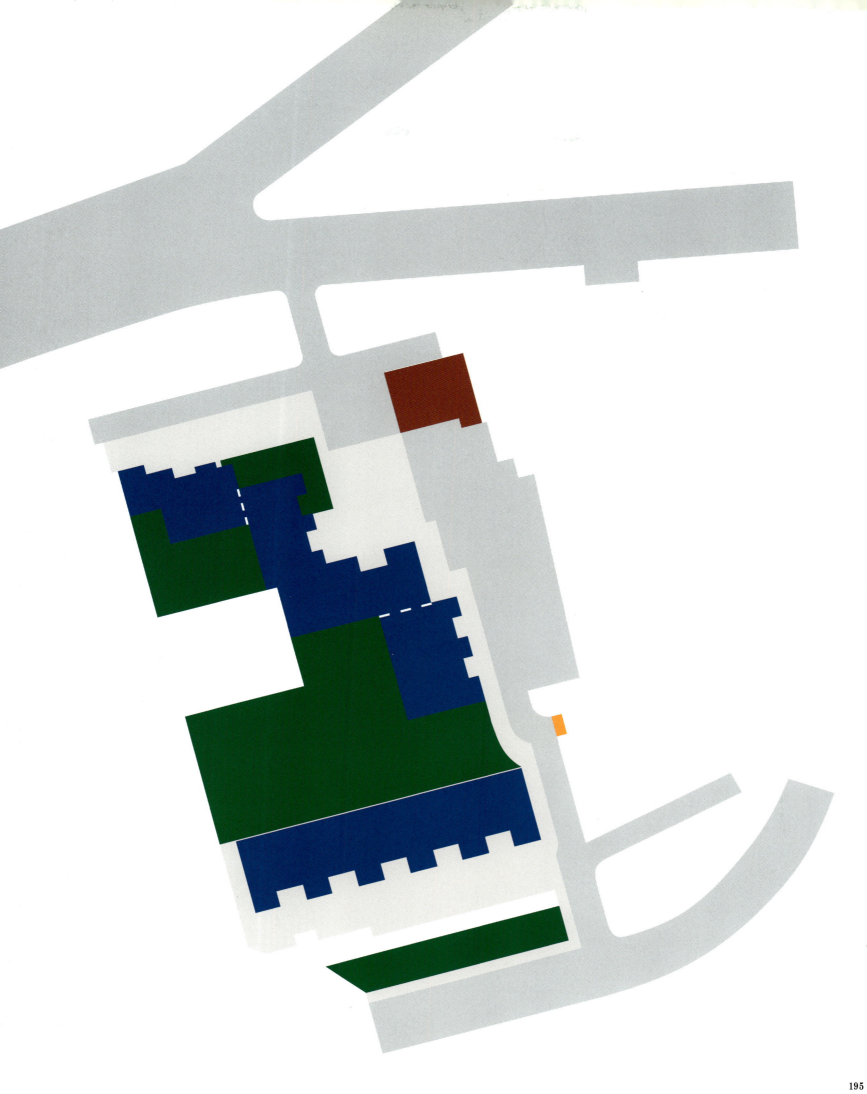

Ladies and gentlemen, this is a stretch of prime English landscape with hills by Samuel Palmer, trees by Constable and sky by JMW Turner. The stream descends from one of the peaks on which fires burned to warn of the approaching Spanish Armada. The collection of mature oaks dates back, at a conservative estimate, to the Napoleonic Wars, and many locals take the haphazard arrangement of large stones to be evidence of an ancient pagan site of worship.

Three British sovereigns have hunted on this land, two prime ministers have fished the river and an archbishop built his house here. The sons and daughters of the vale have given themselves in service to their nation for generations. Agincourt, Waterloo, Ypres, Port Stanley – the roll of fields in which they fell is long, yet throughout, this place has stayed unchanged, a timeless symbol of all that they believed in. Wordsworth's daffodils bloom in the valley each spring, summer is infused with the spirit of Betjeman as long shadows fall across the cricket field, and in autumn Keats's swallows twitter in the skies. This is a first-rate opportunity to claim a piece of England that is 'Jerusalem' and 'Nimrod' brought to life. May we start the bidding please?

Live Pure

Speak True

Right Wrong

Index

All concepts and art direction : Fuel
(unless indicated *)

All pages : Fuel
(unless credited)

Contributors

Peter Anderson
97, 102-103, 106-107, 114*

Philip-Lorca diCorcia
70-71*, 178-179*

Matthew Donaldson
Front and back cover
168-169, 171, 172, 175

Annabel Elston
34 bl, br, 37 tl, bl, 41, 44-48, 51, 62-63,
65, 66, 74 tl, bl, 77 b, 92-93, 98, 110,
153, 159, 188-189, 193, 204

Toby Glanville
136*, 182-183*

Hugo Glendinning
35*, 36*, 38-39*

Frances Gransden
78*, 108-109*, 154*

Michael Grant
129*, 202-203*

Clifton Hepburn
42-43, 49, 55, 105, 124,
127, 130

Anthony Lawrence
75, 80

Bertien van Manen
137*, 160-165*

David Moore
144-149*

Fleur Olby
113, 121

Mike Smith
81

David Spero
6-7*, 26-27*, 186, 190-191, 194

Juergen Teller
94*

Pages 11-25, history section written by Liz Farrelly,
photographed by Trevor Ball

Pages 102-107, pinstriped boilersuit made by Timothy Everest.
Worn by Dr Jeremy Gledhill with Esme Anderson, Mick Sanders,
Cynthia Inions, Andrew Elliott

Page 104, quotes from Sebastian Horsley

Page 125, recycled plastic supplied by Jane Atfield for Made of Waste
Chair manufactured by Oval Workshop

Pages 134-135, image reproduced by Gordon Murray

Page 161, caption written by Bertien Van Manen

Page 171, smile by Aurelia Donaldson

Page 198, handwriting by Gladys Sarjeant